Inspiration Te★as Style

Inspiration Te★as Style

Wyman Meinzer

Introduction by John Graves

Badlands Blue Star Publications, LLC

Copyright © 2008 Badlands Blue Star Publications, LLC

All rights reserved. No portion of this book may be reproduced in any form or by any means, including electronic storage and retrieval systems, except by explicit prior written permission of the publisher except for brief passages excerpted for review and critical purposes.

This book is typeset in Adobe Garamond Pro. The paper used in this publication is acid free and meets the minimum requirements of the American National Standard for Permanence of Paper for Printed Library Materials Z39.48-1992.

Book and cover design by Jerod Foster
Endleaf: Chinati Sunset, Marfa, Texas

08 09 10 11 12 13 14 15 16 / 9 8 7 6 5 4 3 2 1

Library of Congress Cataloging Data available.

ISBN 978-0-9798907-0-3 (cloth : alk. paper)

Badlands Blue Star Publications, LLC
Box 195
Benjamin, Texas 79505
contact@badlandsdesign.com
www.badlandsdesign.com

Printed in China

Dedicated to the past generations of people whose independent spirits
define the Texas we know today.

Preface

In the eyes of many young Texans today, my generation is often considered "the older ones," those baby boomers whose parents were born in the World War I era, survived the Depression years, some in tents and dugouts, and then engaged in that great consolidated effort that won World War II, giving that wonderful age group the much deserved title of the Greatest Generation.

My youth, in the late 1950s through the 1960s, was spent with a rifle in hand and running largely unrestrained on horseback or afoot throughout the hills and canyons along the Brazos river in the Texas Rolling Plains on a forty-section ranch managed by my father, an old-time cowboy whose education was largely measured by the number of worn out saddles to his credit instead of hours spent in the school room. Our hometown, some eleven miles from the ranch house, was Benjamin, the county seat, harboring a population at that time of about 325 folks, principally of farm and ranch origin. The entire region was of a rough complexion, known historically as a place hard on man and beast, and once described by nineteenth-century explorer, Randolph Marcy, as "a land that I doubt will be inhabited into the next century." This was my part of Texas that I grew to know from early childhood, along with its fauna, history and the old generation of people who helped settle it. Quite early in life, I exhibited a definite sense of place and showed little reservation in expressing the love that I had for this land.

For a young boy with a dog, rifle and adventurous inclinations, the ragged old badlands of that region offered a unique learning environment. With a good number of the "old ones" still alive to answer questions about a younger land before my time and a region rich in its offering of indigenous natural fauna and historical happenings, I had a ready curriculum in archeology, geology, history and wildlife behavior all rolled in one. To this impressionable and inquisitive youngster one could say the land afforded me with a rare hands-on learning environment much more interesting than the school rooms at Benjamin ISD. As one might guess, I became an astute and attentive student in this natural classroom and molded well to the ways of this region.

Although of fighting age during a portion of the Vietnam era, I was enrolled at Texas Tech University studying Wildlife Management during the tail end of that war and basically won the lottery with my birth date of November 4, 1950, a number that ensured the continuity of my college education during those uncertain times. After graduating in 1974 with a Bachelor of Science degree in Range and Wildlife Management, I retreated back to the canyon lands along the Wichita and Brazos Rivers to continue my pursuit in studying and hunting the wild canids whose presence was cause for a fascination that held me in an unrelenting grip and helped fuel my interest in the land and history of this piece of Texas.

By the mid-1970s, I'd begun to develop an above average interest in the photographic medium. Despite my upbringing in a "rough hewn" environment, I'd always been aware of a creative streak in my personality that was often a cause to drop whatever at hand to study the color of a sunset, the structure of a thunderstorm, or just the play of subtle light on the facial lines of a given few from our Greatest Generation. With time, the maturation process of seeing would shape my need for visual expression and in turn provide the energy for a quarter-century race to experience the high tide of adventure over a large chunk of America, Canada, and much of Mexico.

In my field of work, I am in constant contact with persons who are gifted by way of the word, brush, camera, or other instruments of choice. The old adage of a connection through tribal affiliation fits well this clan of creative souls. We are sometimes viewed as a strange lot by normal folk as we stumble about our lives seeking an unseen power that might spur our respective expertise into a productive mode. Be it light, weather, landscape, architecture, music, artifical stimulus, or simply a voice from within, if asked what stimulates our creative spirits, I will venture to say that rarely would two people offer an identical answer.

But the ability to recognize an inspirational stimulus is not restricted only to the fraternity of people described above. Some of my greatest work over the past thirty-odd years resulted from the urging of cowboys, ranchers, farm hands, CEOs, political figures, homemakers, and others who had the opportunity and took the time to experience a phenomenon of interest that was cause for that individual to feel a need for self expression. Perhaps through an inability to recognize their own potential to effectively communicate a personal offering, I have often been asked to help channel that creative energy through my own talent and choice of media. I consider this an honor of the highest order.

Although our America is a conglomerate of fifty wonderful states, whose lineage of people, history and geography make our country one of the greatest on the global stage, I must admit that my Texas occupies that special niche in my soul known only to those who were born and reared within these recognizable borders. In this work "Inspiration Texas Style," we have chosen to ask a cross section of Texans to express their own feelings of what this state means to them. Some of these individuals are well known on the world stage while others are salt-of-the-earth beings. In a few cases, verities uttered long ago were from those not born in Texas but came later, their voices echoing a desire for inclusion beneath the title of Texans. By pairing each verbal offering to images collected here, we hope to focus on both the rich visual heritage that our state offers to the American theme and also to recognize a collection of personal prose whose authors possess a definite sense of place. This is Texas as defined from the hearts of Texans.

Wyman Meinzer, 2008

Introduction

Through one family line I am a fourth-generation Texan. I grew up in Fort Worth, worked at summer jobs on farms and ranches, was often in Cuero where my father's people lived, went to college in Houston, hunted and fished up and down the state, and later taught for a time at the University in Austin. Early on, like most of my regional contemporaries, I was happy and proud to be a native, for our generation had had Texas history and chauvinistic lore pumped into us as a part of education, from early grades through high school. And I seem to have been something of a backward-looker from the start, a born retrospective. So were many of my friends.

World War Two began to change things. Before it, the American regions differed from one another far more than they do now, and they stamped those differences on their citizens. This was emphasized in language, in the welter of regional dialects and accents that surrounded us in all branches of the military. A good many of us got to where we could discern approximate origins from the way somebody talked. We were tuned in to such linguistic subtleties as the distinction between a Virginia "ou" and the North Carolina one, or even, some of the time, to the tiny ways in which the form of English that linguists call "Hill Southern" varied in its path from the Appalachians down through a number of states to Texas, and so on.

However, the war's blending of millions on millions of young Americans with one another was hard on regionalistic views and traits, as we came to know and esteem comrades shaped in places whose ways and values contrasted with our own. By the time peace came, the close friends I had made were less often from Texas than from Kentucky, Tennessee, Maine, California, and other segments of the sprawling national map.

When we were all civilians again, most of us went home wherever home was, some to remain and shape their lives in known surroundings, and others not. At first I was one of the latter, but I have examined my own post-war flounderings in my books and will not detail them again — graduate school, college teaching, a failed marriage, literary ambitions that led to published writing but also to a novel that turned out badly, and wide wandering on this continent and abroad. I guess I came to think of myself as a sort of citizen of the world, and I felt a certain satisfaction in having never been known as "Tex" anywhere except in one New York bar near Gramercy Park, where the astute owner detected my twang.

Back then, I had no intention of returning to home grounds except on visits to family and friends. In the late 1950s, though, one such visit was caused by my father's grave illness leading to big surgery, after which I stayed around to be of such help as I could.

That staying around turned out to last for the rest of my life. What happened was that simply being back in Texas revived my youthful fascination with the region and its specific history, landscapes, people, and ways. I found a first-rate, secluded, and little-used Southwestern section in the basement of Fort Worth's old Carnegie Public Library, with a knowledgeable and helpful lady in charge whose name I wish I remembered. The books in her musty domain not only reawakened old interests in me but added to them. And as a writer, I began to use them as material for stories and articles.

My writing up to that point in life, though it had supported me during my geographic ramblings, had not been distinctive except in a few decent short stories and an essay or two. I was well aware of this, especially after that faulty novel, and was still hoping to find my own writing voice somehow. And ironically, where this particular "citizen of the world" did at last work out his voice, whatever its merits, was right back where he had started out, in Texas. He was home, and he liked being there.

I was finding that voice not just in the library's basement bookshelves and in memories, but also in much hunting and fishing and canoeing in places I had known long before. People came into it too, old friends, country folk of sorts I remembered, and ultimately Jane, my beloved wife and my daughters' mother, not a Texan by birth but a well-adapted one by now, having lived with me for most of the last fifty years on the rough and rocky stretch of rural Texas that we call Hard Scrabble.

The voice engendered by all this led to my rather skimpy array of published books, beginning with Goodbye to a River. How their worth as literature will be judged in future times I have no idea, but they are mine. I did my best with them, and I believe all the thrashings and ups and downs of my wandering years may have protected them, at least a little, from the twin vices of provincialism and sentimentality.

And Texas today: what do I think about it?

From one angle, that of a not just aging but aged spectator who is not entranced by change, I look at the state as one more example of the enormous surge toward worldwide sameness that is fast destroying regional and national variations just about everywhere. Those differences in modes of human work, play, manners, language and even appearance have fascinated me forever, and I have come to believe that they not only hold rich and interesting color and drama but are a stout force in the possibility of humankind's endurance on this planet, for as Darwin knew, variety fosters survival.

Increasingly, in Texas as elsewhere, hordes of people dwell in crowded unhandsome cities, work in tall buildings for large impersonal enterprises ("corporate entities" in Newspeak), usually just for the money but sometimes for a sense of accomplishment. Outside the skyscrapers suburbs gnaw their way into countrysides, while crime flourishes about as well as it ever has. Many in our region, perhaps most, speak not Hill Southern but a radio-TV sort of English that closely resembles, I have been told, the neutral patois of Lancaster, Pennsylvania. Increasingly their main joys are derived from electronic gadgetry, high-tech transportation and hobbies, and commercialized, frantically hyped sports that spark jingoism here as well as in the rest of the civilized world and some uncivilized parts to boot.

Nor does there appear to be much prospect for change, but only a near-certainty that the pattern will clone itself everywhere it can. The Texas it is creating I find hard to love.

Or is the above just a blast from a rustic codger inching toward age ninety and getting pretty close to it? Said codger knows well that much of the distinctive Texas that shaped him and finally gave him his voice as a writer is still with us. The rivers, shrunken and fouled as many of them are. The long and curving coast with its estuarial bays, fertile prairies and, farther south, the original Hispanic and Texan ranching terrain chronicled by J. Frank Dobie and others. The damp eastern forests, the Blacklands. The tough beautiful Hill Country, the Rolling Plains where later ranches stand amid their own wealth of cowboy-and-Indian lore. The Llano Estacado, a flat and almost featureless broad steppe except in the canyons of the Caprock escarpment and the Canadian River valley, but beloved by those it has bred. And beyond there the magnificently jumbled and arid Trans-Pecos with its Big Bend. I have known and cared about all these areas, along with their differing kinds of Texans, for many of whom Hill Southern is still the dialect of choice, inherited from their forebears and backed up, these days, by the country music that blares from jukeboxes and radios and disk-players wherever one goes.

They are still here, these diverse regions, though there has been a great deal of abusive alteration of their lands, waters, vegetation, and wildlife. Texans who see such ills with clear eyes have grown more and more inclined to do something about them, to resist further hostile changes and, where possible, to rectify the damage already done. I am on their side, if not always with optimism.

Some of the cities, despite my ranting about them, still have a bit of regionality in their ways, a touch of Texanness, especially the older, retrospective ones like San Antonio and El Paso. Towns along the Rio Grande border and near it continue to exude their own special Tex-Mex aura, though they also possess an assortment of current troubles related to our times and to the *otro lado* across the river. And all up and down the state, cities — large or small, homogenized or not — have a full share of keen-witted, warm, and interesting people whatever dialect they speak, and nurture colleges, museums, parks, good hospitals, and other amenities that, yes, even such countrified and backward-minded oldsters as myself have to like, or anyhow approve.

So yes, too, I'm content to have been shaped by old Texas as a youngster and to live here in my latter years. It is home. It is mine, changes and all. Whatever its future may be, it is where I belong.

John Graves
"Texas, A Personal View," 2008

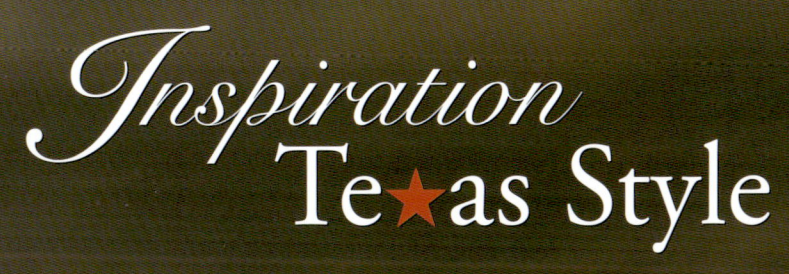

Nowhere in the world is there a place to match Texas. Whether in the beauty of its land, the majesty of its skies, or the strengths of its people, Texas is unique.

John Cornyn
United States Senator

The people make Texas the great state that it is. There are more leaders and unique people in Texas than in any other state in the nation.

Boone Pickens
Entrepreneur

A voice says, "Cry out."
And I said, "What shall I cry?"
"All men are like grass, and all their glory is like the flowers of the field."

                        Isaiah 40:6

Texas is history.
It's the rough and tough settlers that made their homes here.
It's the respect Texans show for their past and present, and it's the dedication of all to keep our state unique and genuine.

Tom Perini
Perini Ranch Steakhouse

Where were you when I laid the earth's foundation?
Tell me, if you understand.
Who marked off its dimensions? Surely you know!
Who stretched a measuring line across it?
On what were its footings set, or who laid its cornerstone – while the morning stars sang together and all the angels shouted for joy?

Job 38: 4-7
Inspiration for Ellen McStay, Texan

I make no more calculations except to spend my life here, rich or poor, here I expect to remain permanently.

Stephen F. Austin
Father of Texas

Texas is big!
The only thing bigger than Texas
is the hearts of all Texans.
I am proud to be a Texan.

Tom Bivins
Rancher

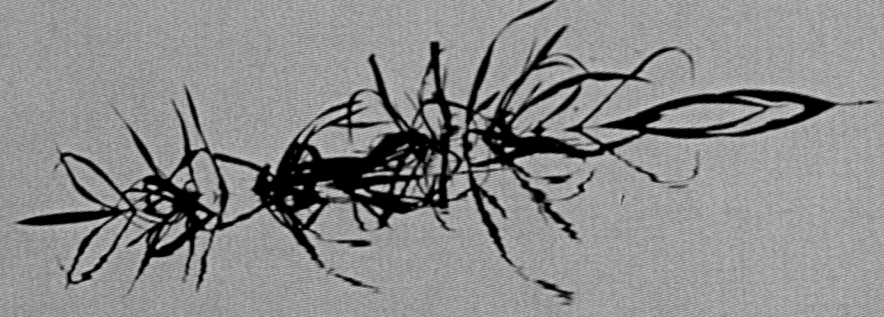

Overleaf:

The great State of Texas is a blessing and a land of opportunity for everyone.

Don Haskins
College Basketball Coach

Texas is nothing but an idea:
an idea of openness, an idea of horizon,
an idea of unlimited sky.

Andy Wilkinson
Poet and Songwriter

Texas is more than a state; it is a state of mind. Texans are independent, passionate and loyal people, fiercely dedicated to those causes that most stir their hearts. Our people comprise a rich tapestry of races, creeds and cultures that makes ours a state unlike any other. Dwelling in a diversity of settings ranging from the stark beauty of Big Bend to the piney woods of East Texas, our citizens are rightfully proud of the Lone Star State. Because we are so blessed, I truly mean it when I say, "God bless the great State of Texas."

Rick Perry
Governor of Texas

The Texas outdoors is a vast resource with room for everyone;
all she asks is a little respect from those of us who venture forth.

David Baxter
Consulting Editor, Texas Wildlife

Texas will again lift its head and stand among nations. It ought to do so, for no country upon the globe can compare with it in natural advantages.

Sam Houston
President of the Republic of Texas

Overleaf:

He opened the rock, and the waters gushed out;
they ran in dry places like a river.

Psalm 105:41

I have so much pride for this state. . .
When I address a letter, I refuse to abbreviate the word TEXAS.
I spell it out!

Kynn Patterson
Rancher

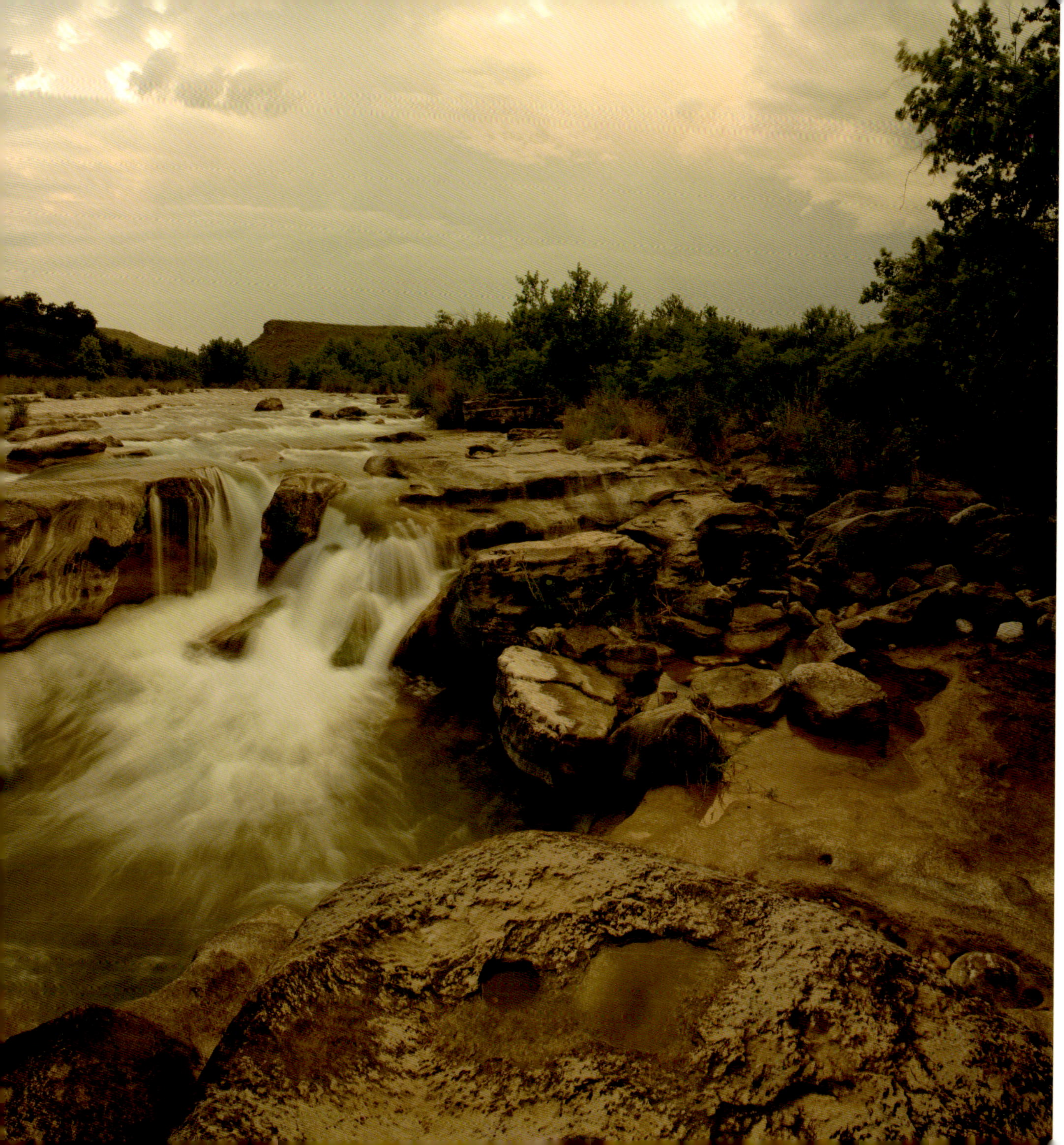

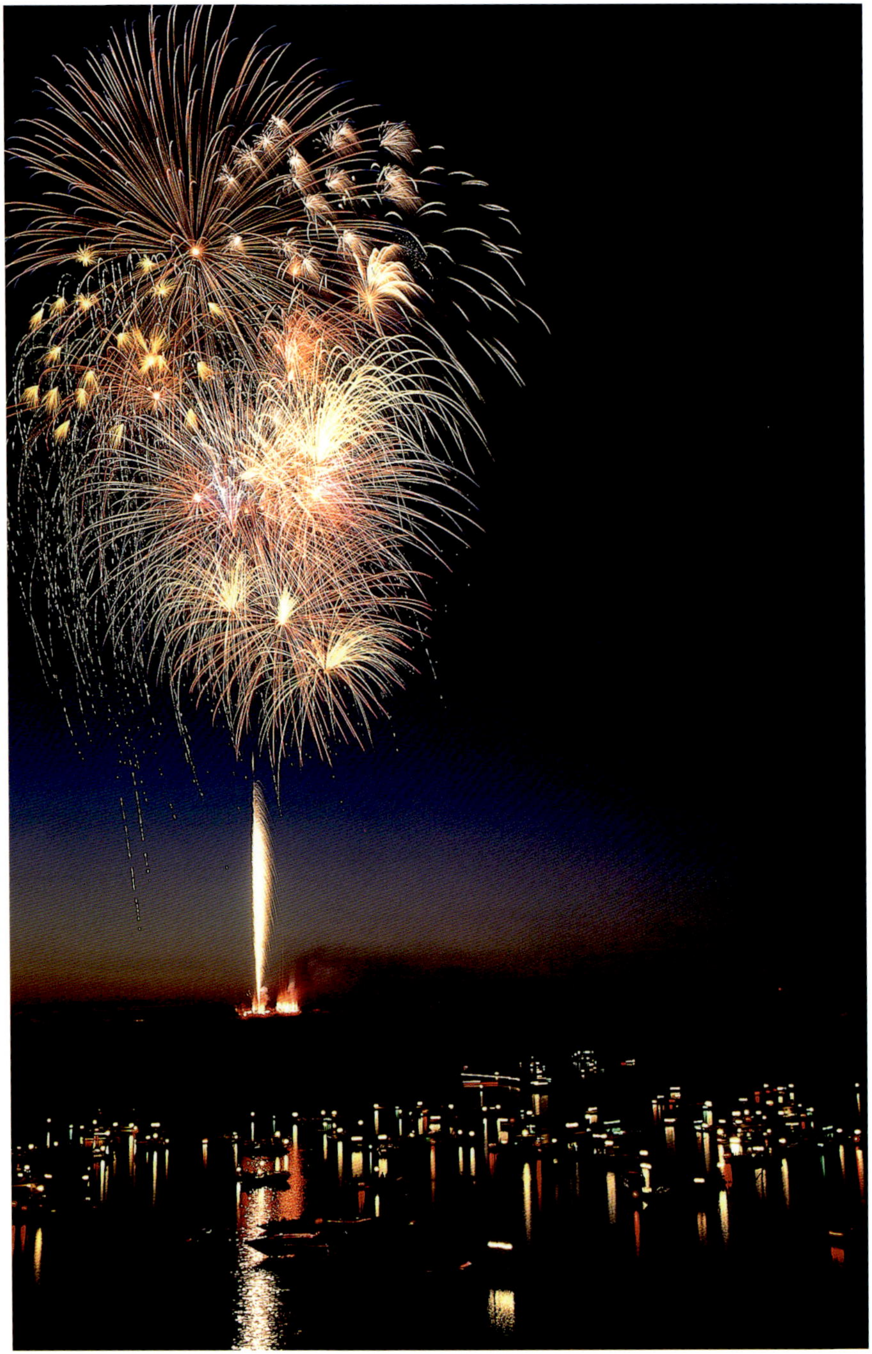

If you love America you should understand the love for Texas. From our beaches to our mountains, our dry streams to our big rivers, our deserts to our forests, our alligators to our big horn sheep, our one horse towns to our cities, our unique cultures to our diversity, our villains to our heroes, our history to our future. Everything Texas *is* America in one big, beautiful state. My kids are fifth-generation Texans, and they understand; Texas is America – concentrated.

W.H. (Bucky) Wharton
Rancher, Waggoner Ranch

Overleaf:

We focus so much on what we're waiting for that we miss or forget to appreciate what we have.

Tom Butler
Cowboy, Forever 18

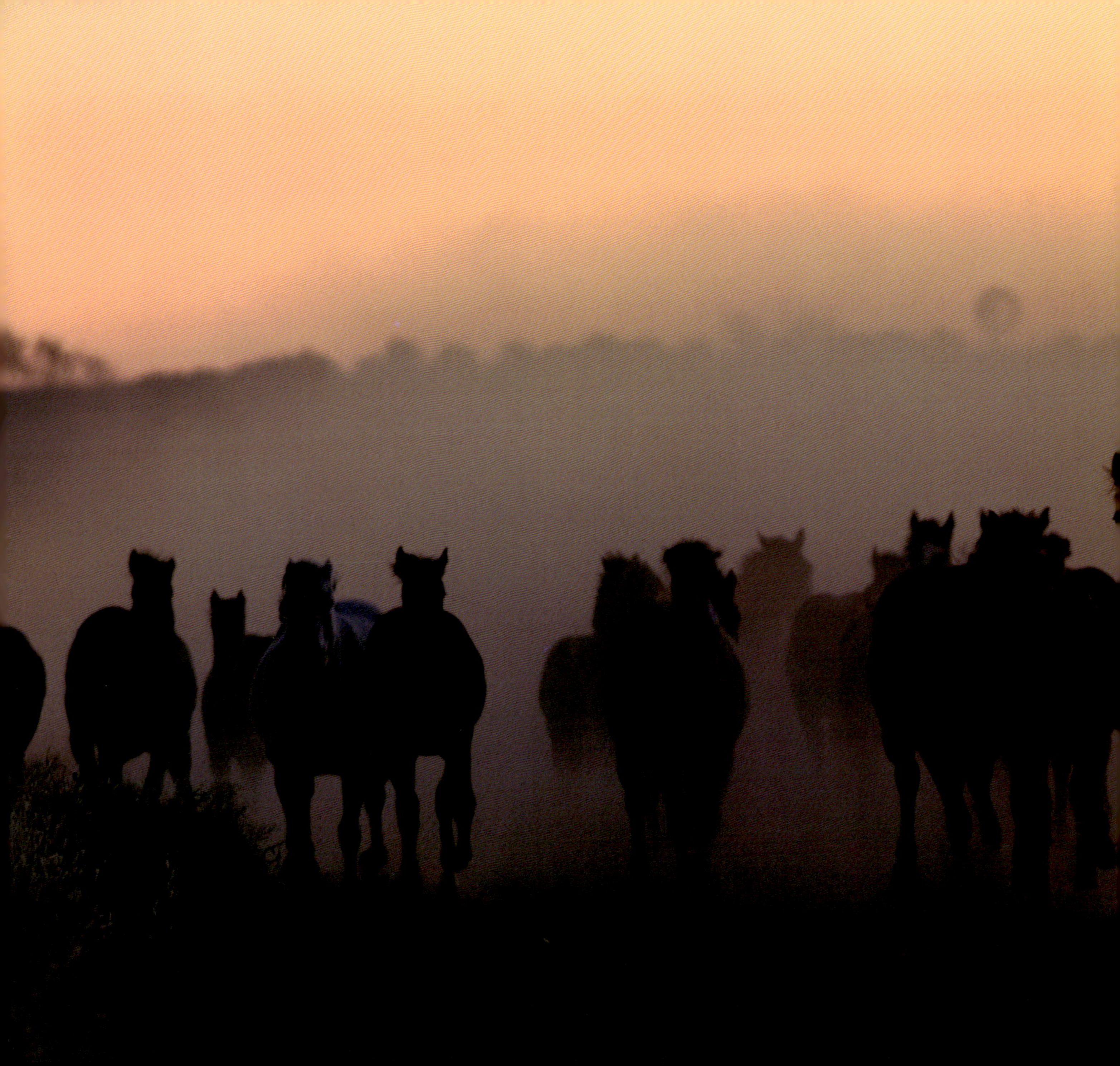

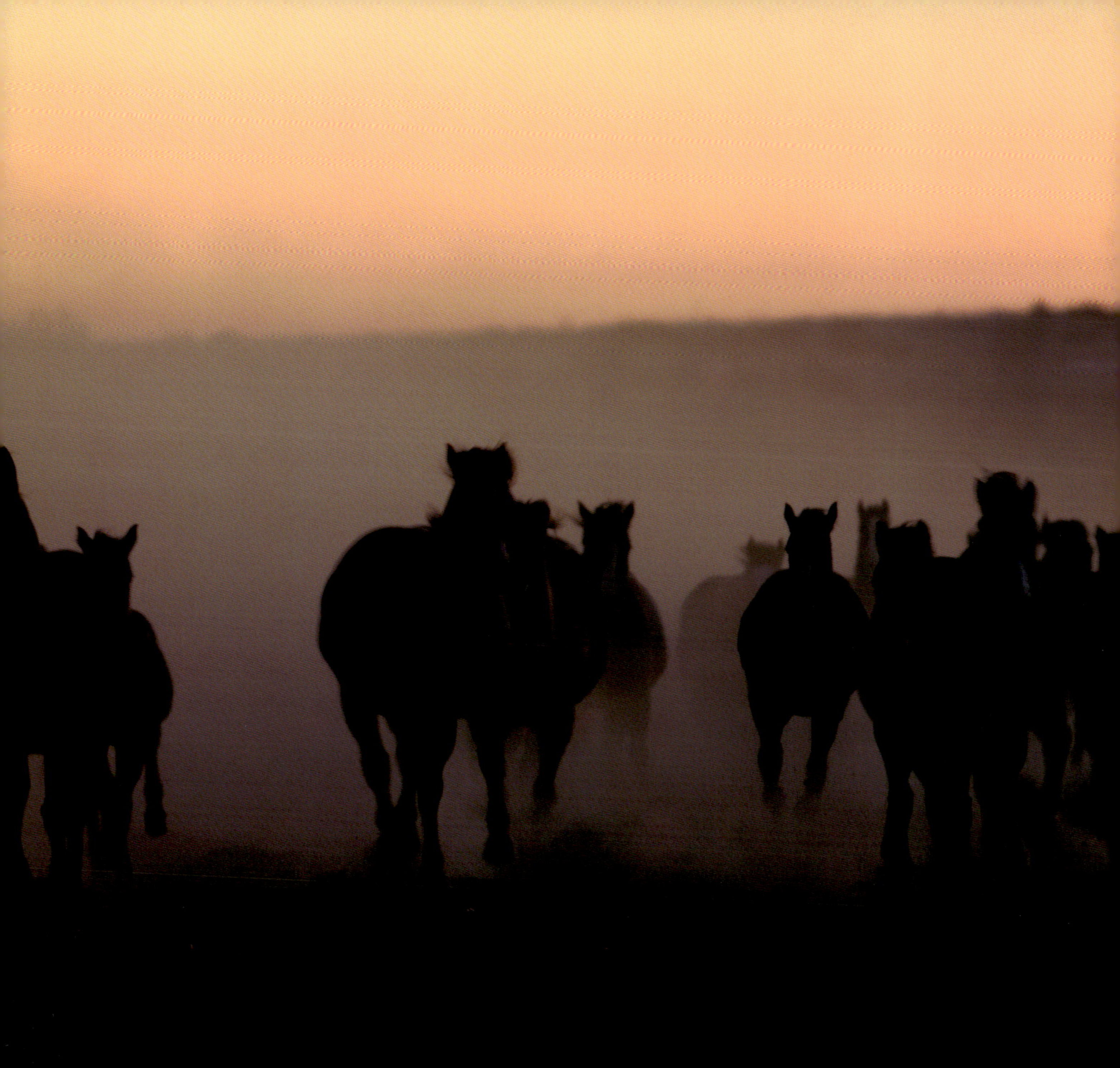

If I hadn't been born in Texas,
I would have run away from home and come here.

Red McCombs

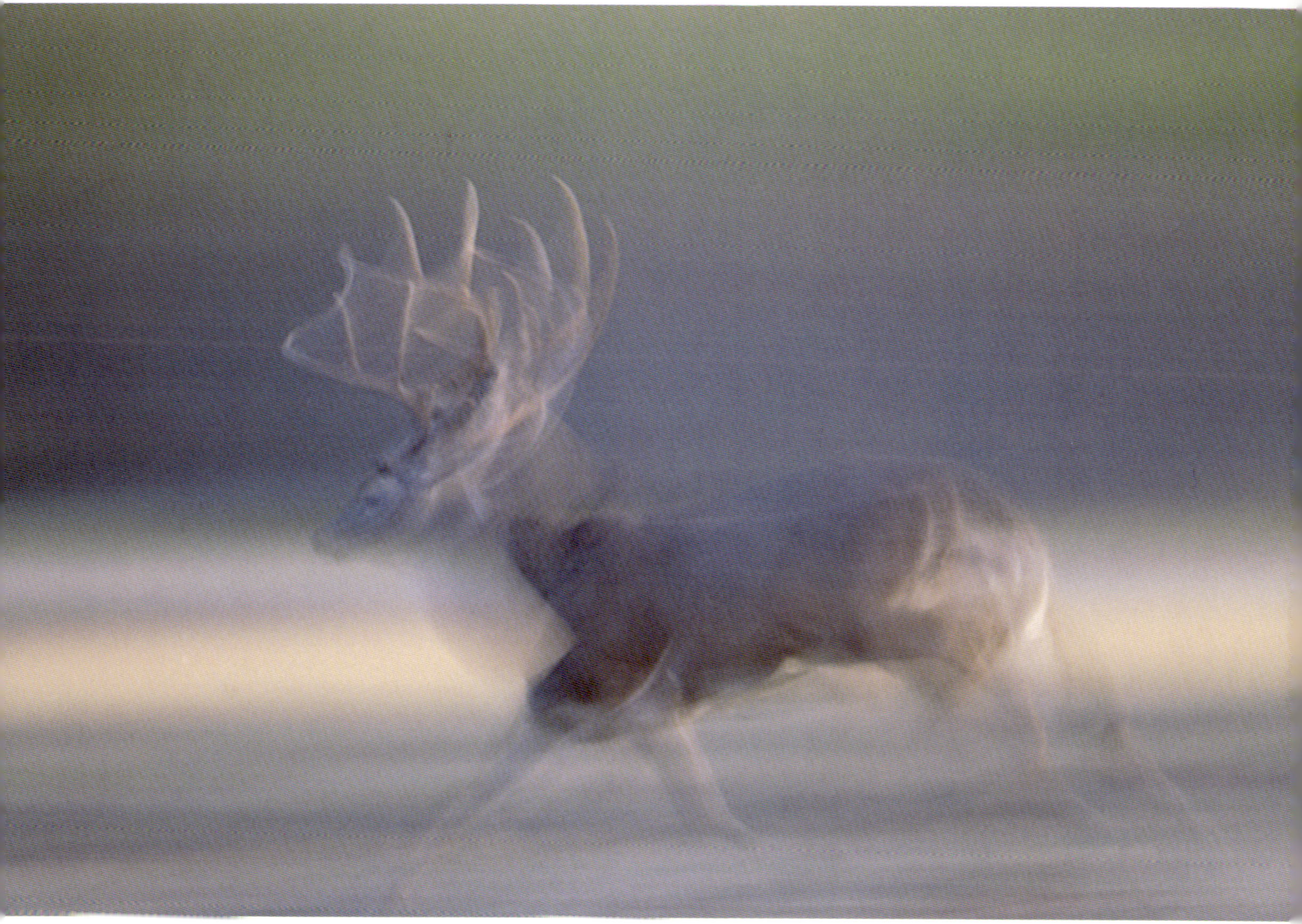

My ears had heard of you,
but now my eyes have seen you.

Job 42:5
Inspiration for Becky Holt, Texan

Texas is a state of *home*. Texans that are lucky enough to have been born here rarely stay gone for long. Those that weren't so lucky have found their new home very inviting indeed. Because of the strong roots we all put down, we develop and maintain friendships for life. The Panhandle is closer to four other state Capitals than Austin, but we feel more in common with someone from Beaumont than someone from Tucumcari. Texas is one big family!

Mark Bivins
Commissioner, Texas Parks and Wildlife

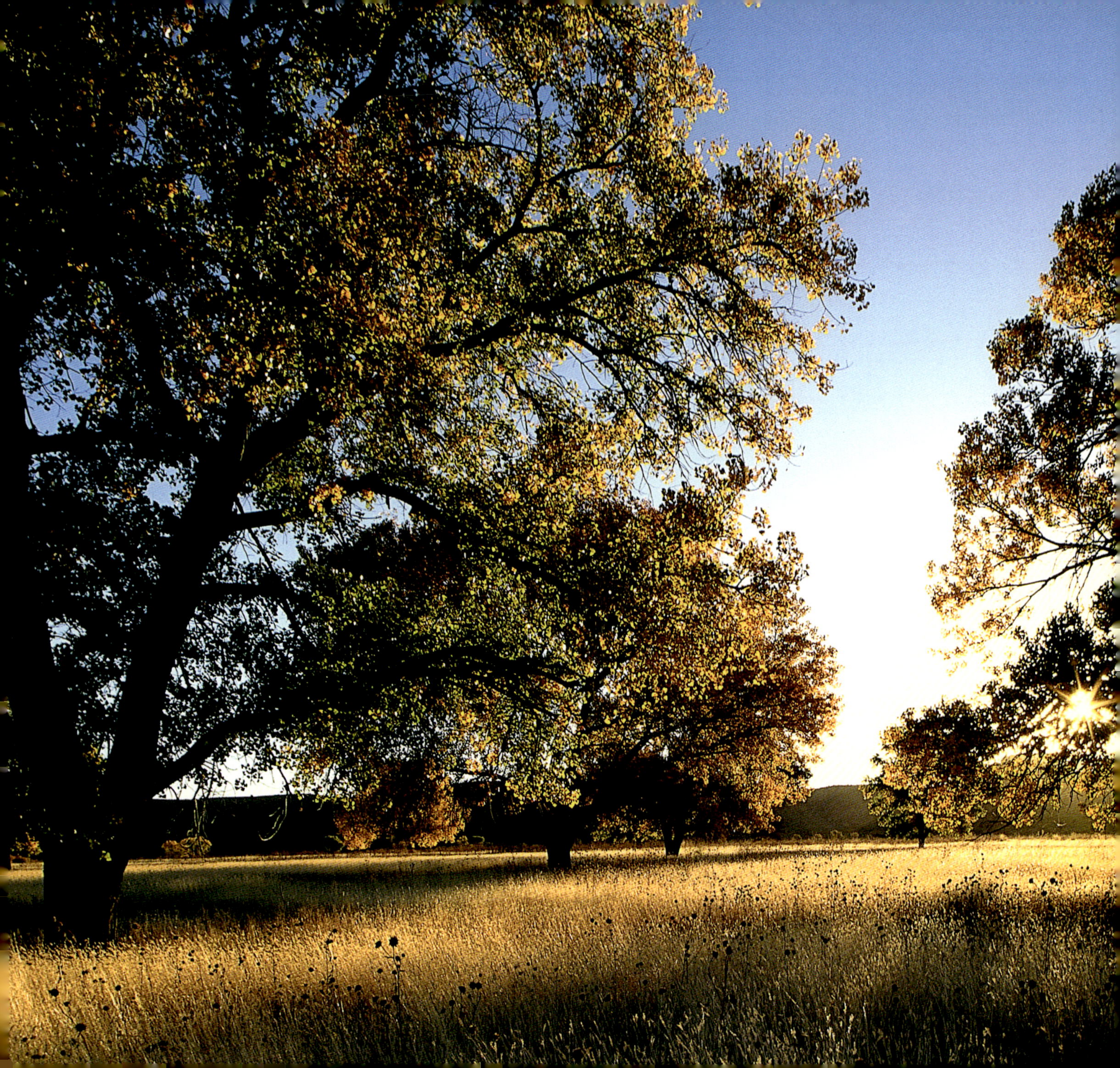

My Texas is space and light.
In it I'm never crowded in body, mind or spirit.

Bryan Woolley
Retired Writer, The Dallas Morning News

Wide open spaces and a rugged landscape crawling with tenacious life define West Texas. The region's flatlands, canyonlands and mountains from the Panhandle Plains to the Big Bend bring visual and visceral adventures. Red bluffs and an ever-changing and magnetic sky allow solitude, where the earth becomes a loyal companion.

Kippra D. Hopper
Author and Photographer

The University of Texas is a microcosm of Texas itself; proud and assertive, complex and unique. For centuries past and centuries to come, Texas has been a crossroads of the energies and aspirations that foster success.

William C. Powers, Jr.
President, The University of Texas at Austin

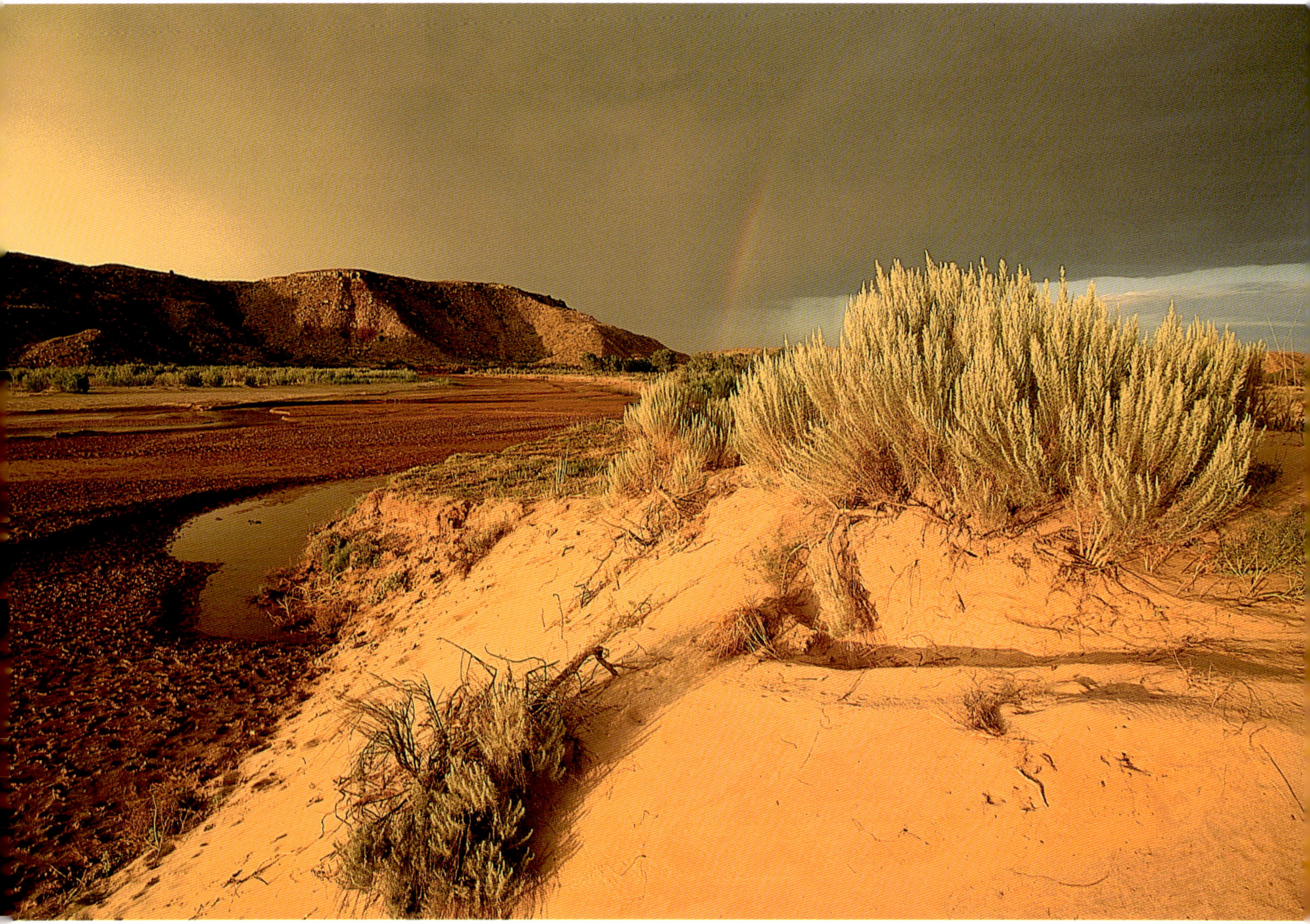

Texas is outrageous. It is not just a place, rather it has magical qualities that transcend space and time. From its earliest days as a Republic, and then statehood, it has offered its people the hope of a bountiful harvest, unrelenting challenges, the promise of an exciting tomorrow, and boundless opportunity. None other is like it.

John McStay
Texan

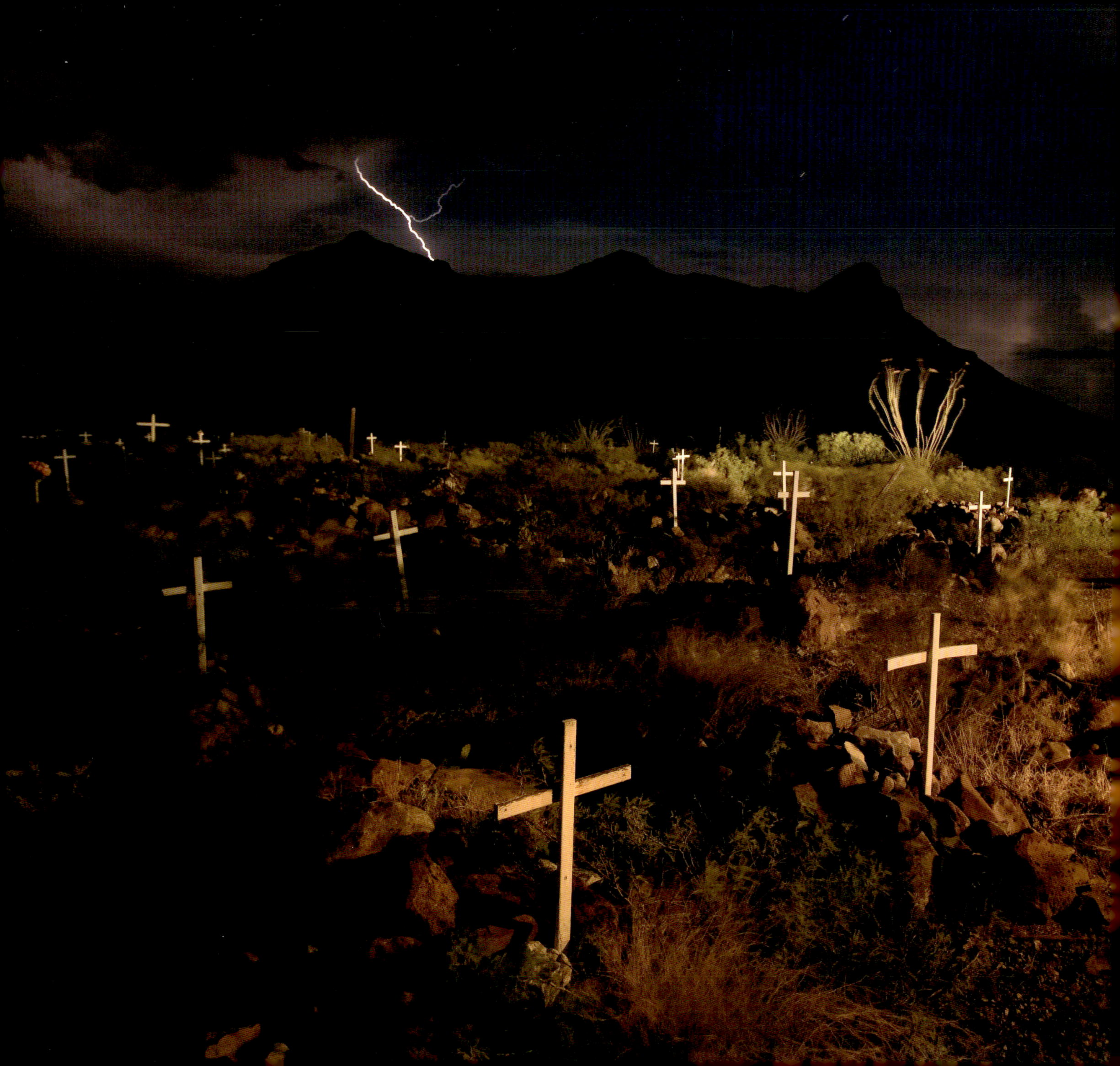

The sting of the grave, the fierceness of the lightening . . . The Victory of the Cross.

Cody Cochran
Cowboy Preacher

Being horseback at breaking dawn, the sound of cattle bawling at the gathering in springtime, the smoke rising from mesquite wood heating the branding irons, dinner at the chuck wagon, poetry around a hay bale circle by a campfire, and a visit to the Modern Art Museum on a Sunday afternoon. That's what I like about Texas.

Ron Hall
Art Dealer
Co-Author of The New York Times *Bestseller,*
"Same Kind of Different As Me"

No matter what corner of this magnificent state I photograph, every unique vista becomes a memorable old friend that stays in my mind's eye and heart always.

Earl Nottingham
Chief Photographer, Texas Parks and Wildlife

suspended except by a vote of at least two
of the members present. Nor shall the order
of business as established by the rules of the house
be postponed or changed except by a vote of at
least two thirds of the members present.

7. It shall be in order for the committee on
enrolled bills to report at any time.

8. No person shall be permitted to pass
within the bar in the chamber occupied by
the convention unless with the consent of
the President.

On Mr Collinsworth's motion Mr
Mr Willis A. Faris was allowed to take a seat at
the secretary's table to note and report the proceedings
of the convention.

Mr Rusk introduced the following resolution
to wit. Resolved that a committee be appointed
consisting of one member from each Municipality
represented in the convention for the purpose of drafting
a constitution for Texas, and that the same be reported as soon as practicable to this body, to be
read and adopted. Whereupon the President proceeded
to appoint Messrs Potter, Stewart, Wallace,
Coleman, Fisher, S Menton, Carson, Johnson, Rusk,
Byrom, Bowie, Everitt, Hardiman, Stapp,
Langford, West, Power, Navarro, McKinney, Hens-
ley, Motley and Menard a committee as afore-
said.

The committee to whom was assigned the
duty of drafting a Declaration of Independence, reported through their Chairman Mr Childress their
Declaration of Independence that will befitting

follow, and moves that the same be entered on the
convention as this report.

Mr Houston moves that the report be amended
by the convention which on being seconded was
done.

On Mr Collinsworth's motion seconded, the House
resolved itself into a committee of the whole upon the
report of the committee on independence.

Mr Collinsworth was called to the chair where
upon Mr Houston introduced the following, resolution, Resolved that the Declaration of Independence reported by the committee be adopted, that
the same be engrossed, and signed by the delegates
of this convention, and the question being put the
resolution was unanimously adopted.

The Unanimous
Declaration of Independence
made by the Delegates of the People
of Texas, in general Convention, at
the town of Washington, on the
2d day of March 1836.

When a government has ceased
to protect the lives, liberty and property of the people,
from whom its legitimate powers are derived, and for
the advancement of whose happiness it was instituted,
and so far from being a guarantee for the enjoy-
ment of those inestimable and inalienable rights,
becomes an instrument in the hands of evil rulers for their
oppression.

When the federal Republican Constitution of
their country which they have sworn to support, no
longer has a substantial existence, and the whole
nature of their government, has been forcibly changed,

The story of Texas has been kept alive by our culture that continues to put forth brave men and women that fill the ranks. For me, it is always easy to explain why most Texans act the way they do when it comes to boasting about this great state. Our history has shaped and taught us what has come about since the actions of selfless men in 1836.

Jose Esparza
Veteran, Iraq Theater

The soul of Texas is its spirit. Action, courage, optimism, and integrity provide the foundation for the future, where discovery, innovation, and opportunity will be our state's gift to society.

Kenneth M. Jastrow II

Nothing is better for a man's land than the shadow of his own soul upon the land (there is no substitute for being there).

Tio Kleberg
Rancher, King Ranch

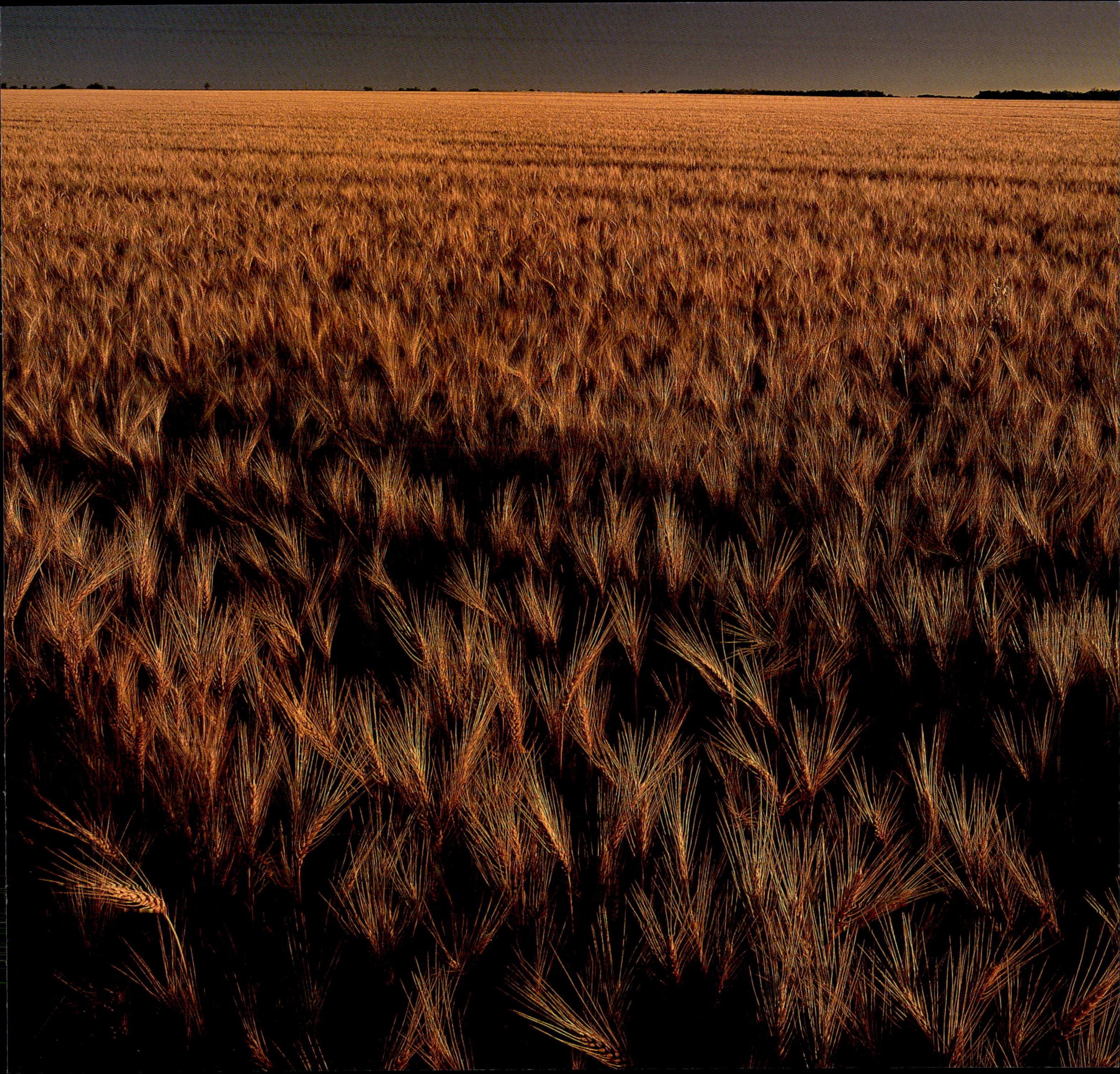

What I like about Texas is the people and their "can do" attitudes. Everywhere you look there are endless opportunities for anyone who will dare to dream, have self-discipline, and are not afraid to work.

David Counts
Former Texas State Representative

The harvest truly is great, but the labourers are few: pray ye therefore the Lord of the harvest, that He would send forth labourers into His harvest.

Luke 10:2

To the People of Texas and all Americans in the world –

Fellow citizens and compatriots – I am besieged by a thousand or more of the Mexicans under Santa Anna – I have sustained a continual bombardment and cannonade for 24 hours and have not lost a man – The enemy has demanded a surrender at discretion, otherwise, the garrison are to be put to the sword if the fort is taken – I have answered the demand with a cannon shot, and our flag still waves proudly from the walls – I shall never surrender or retreat. Then, I call on you in the name of liberty, of patriotism, and everything dear to the American character, to come to our aid with all dispatch – The enemy is receiving reinforcements daily and will no doubt increase to three or four thousand in four or five days. If this call is neglected, I am determined to sustain myself as long as possible and die like a soldier who never forgets what is due to his own honor and that of his country – VICTORY OR DEATH.

William Barrett Travis
Lt. Col. Comdt., February 24, 1836

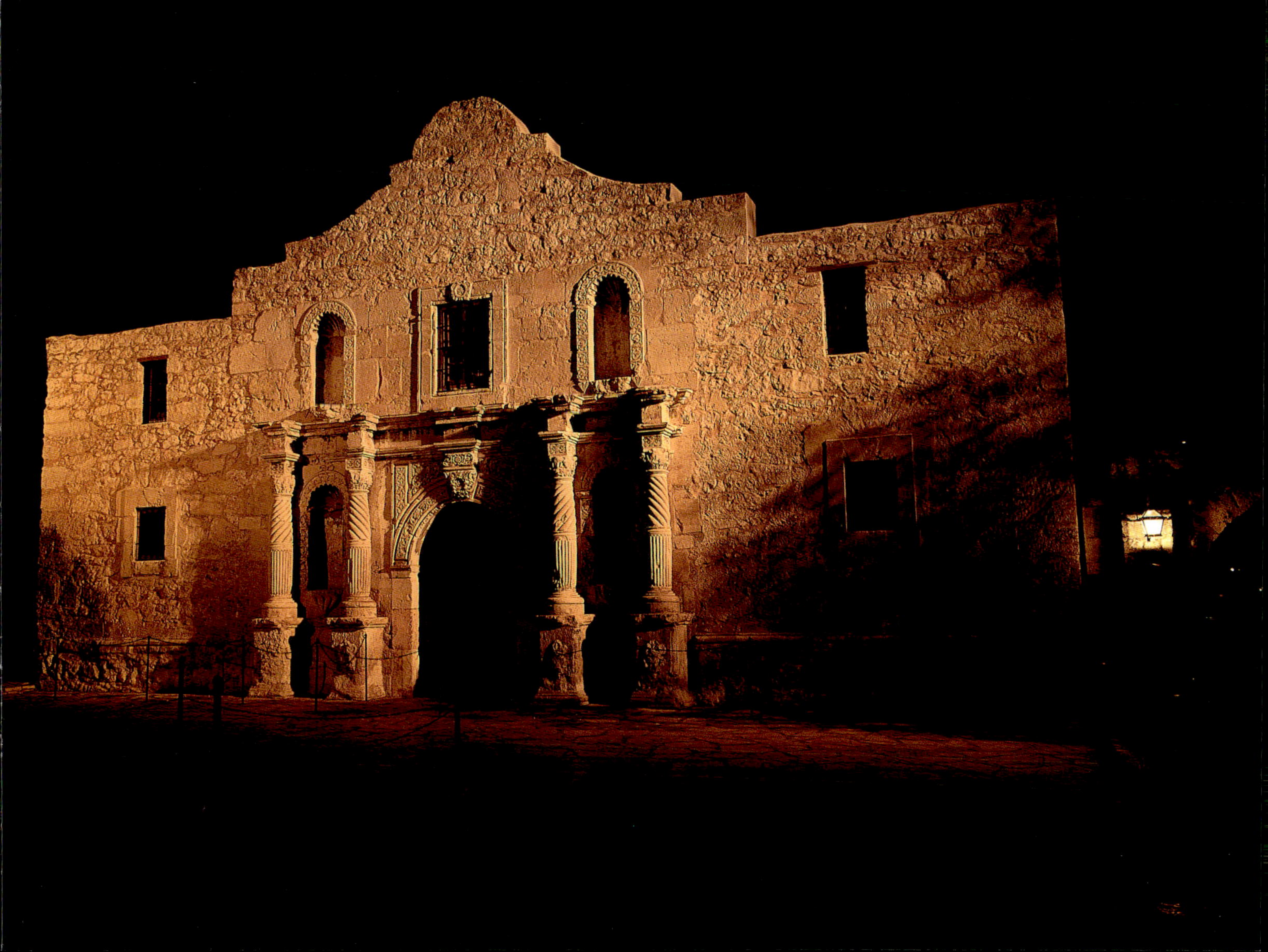

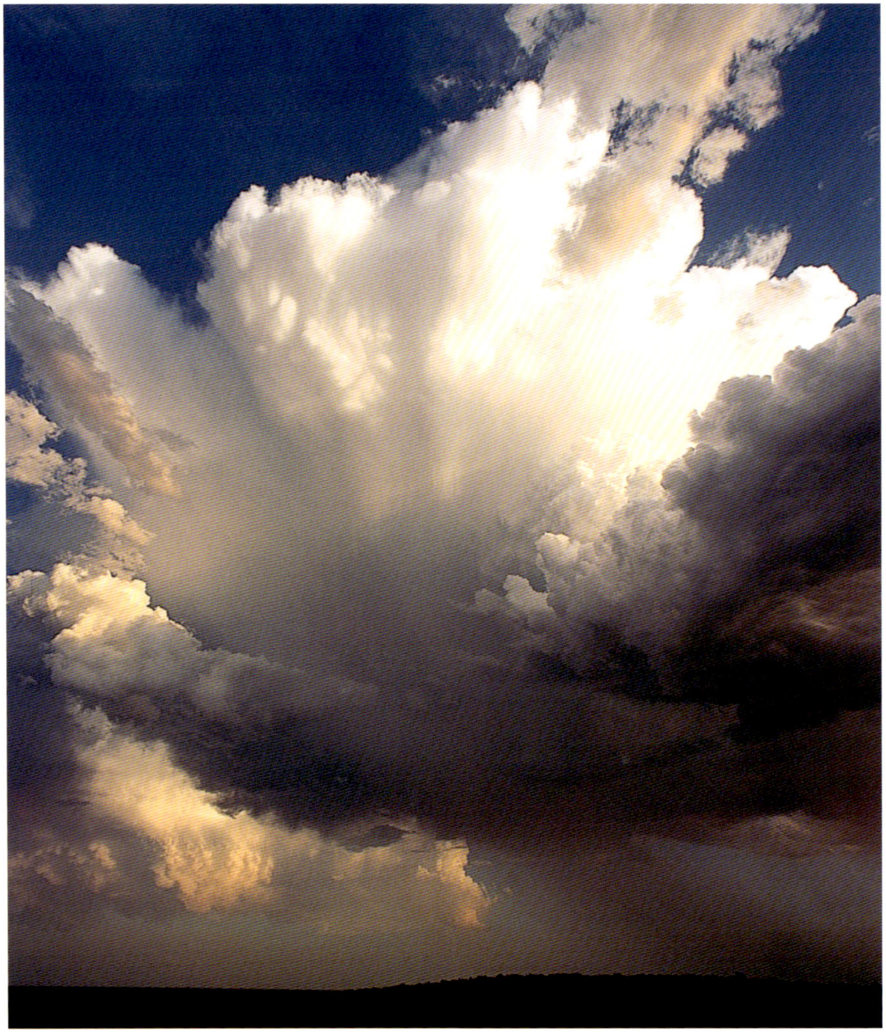

I am the child, and Texas is a vital organ of mankind.
It serves father and mother united of one heart that pulses past birth,
through life and beyond death, as it was at the Alamo and since.
This coursing blood is stirred by love itself.
It will forever inhabit our soul chambers and rise to the call of serving honor,
wild purity, and the cleaner sanctuaries of Texas, our home attached to Heaven.

Tibb Burnett
Texas Poet

Delving into the events of Texas' history is as exhilarating as inhaling the fresh, cool air after a Panhandle rain. The first breath, like finding each new bit of history, leaves me yearning for more.

Alvin Lynn
Geologist, Archaeologist and Historian

Texas – there's no other place for me. Blood, sweat and tears of ancestors have been poured into this soil since 1835. Longhorns, armadillos, cowboys and cacti are what we are, and we fly the Lone Star as high as the Stars and Bars. We gave the Union the greatest state – Texas.

Jack Glover
Cowboy Museum, Wimberly, Texas

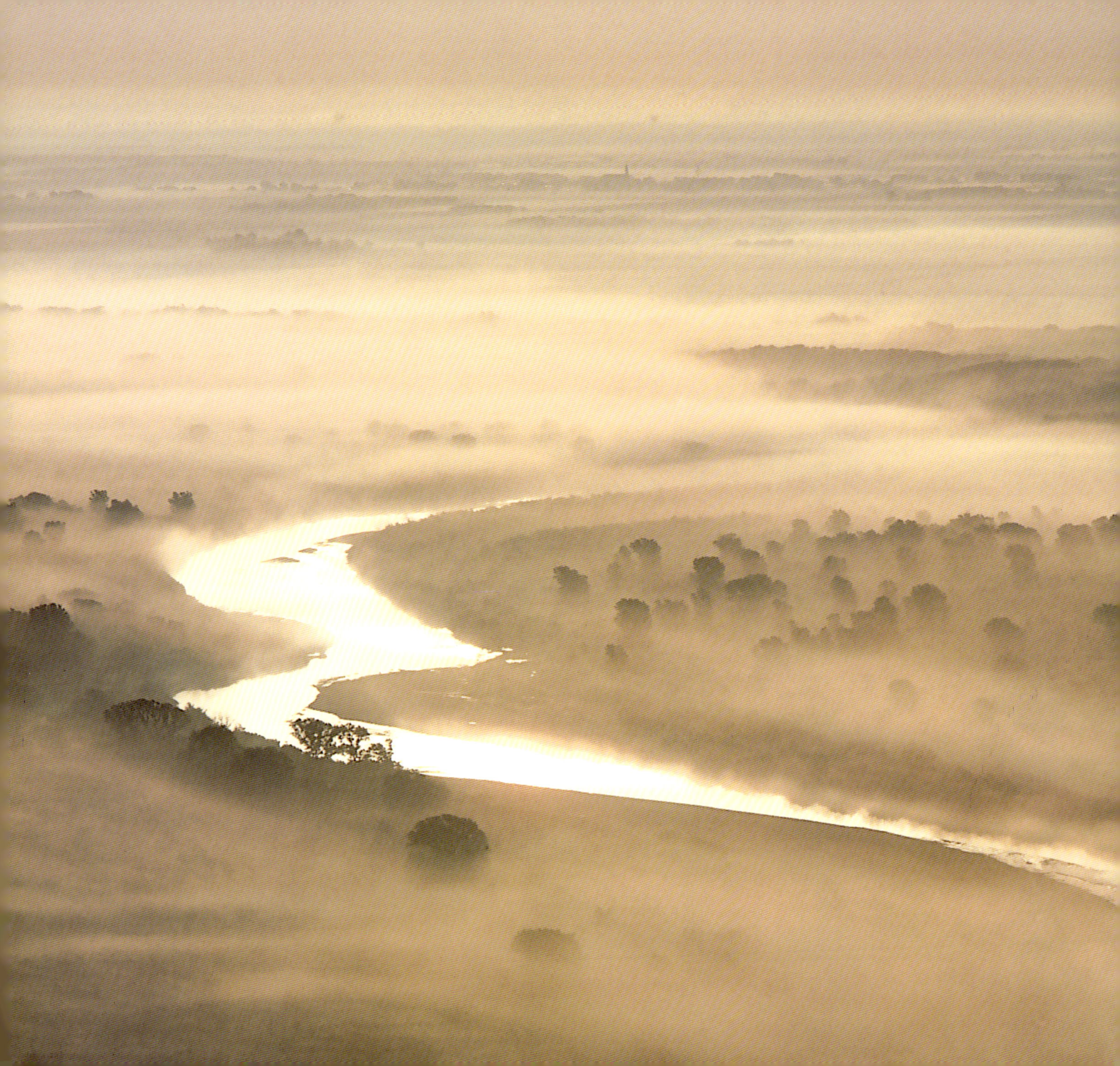

I'm real fond of the area of North Texas explored by Captain R. B. Marcy (5th U.S. Infantry) in 1854, Fort Belknap and parts west. It still has a little bit of wild in it.

Craig Estes
Texas State Senator

In West Texas, our Llano Estacado serves like a palette for what I like to call "participatory geography." We live on a vast canvas of magnificent sunrises and sunsets, of starry nights, and thrilling thunderstorms. Each is unique, and thereby hangs the admonition to participate. Each is to be enjoyed for itself alone; no lounging in the recliner, we are called on to be a part of the wonder around us.

Jim Brink, PhD
Associate Vice Provost for Heritage Consortium for the Natural and Historic Southwest
Executive Director of the Southwest Collection/Special Collections Library

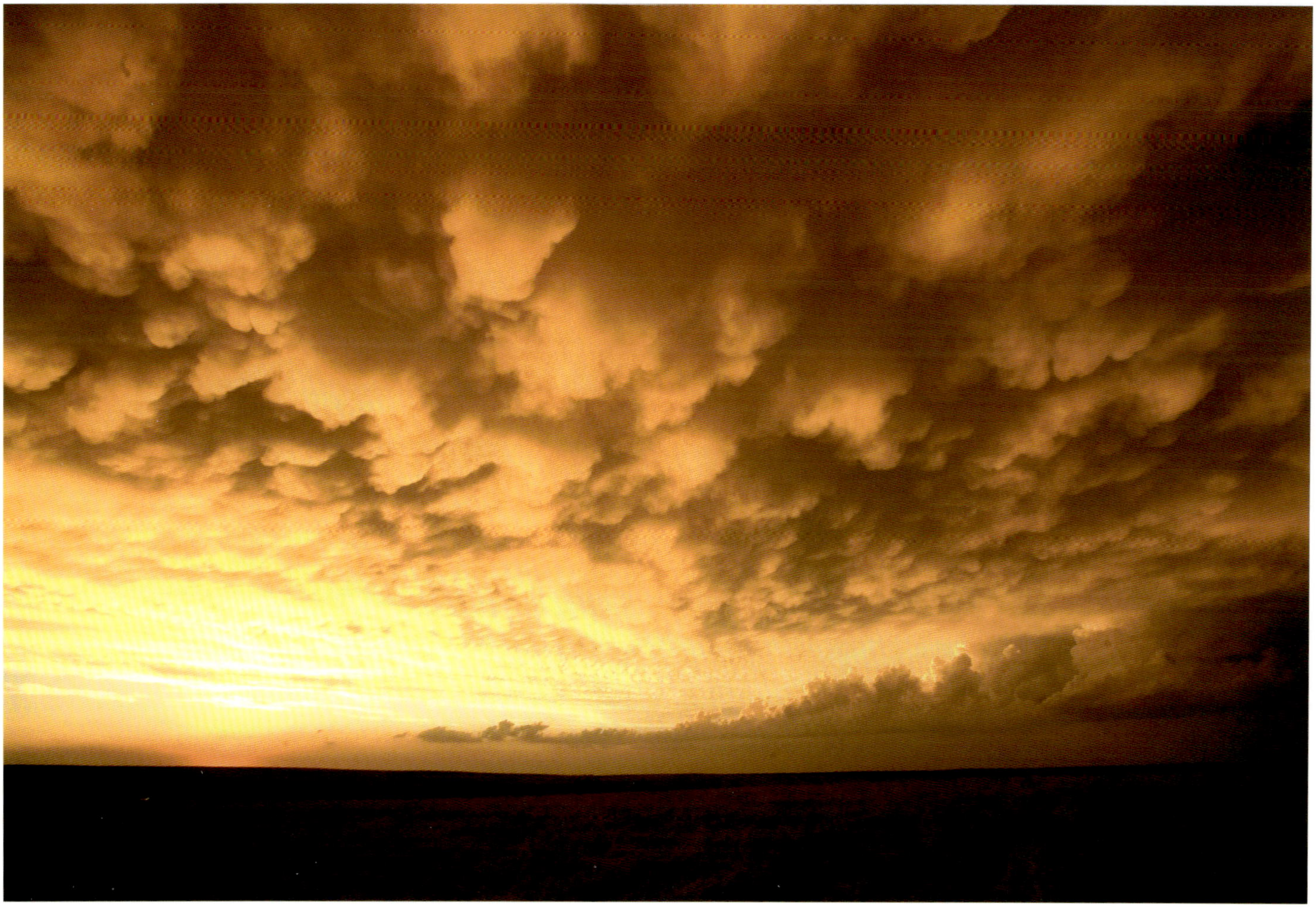

Every time I see the American Flag, and more especially the Texas Flag, I am reminded of the impact my father's teachings on patriotism have had on my life. And when I hear the national anthem or "Texas, Our Texas" played, I am filled with an overwhelming sense of pride for country and my beloved home: The Great State of Texas!

Sylinda Hunter-Meinzer
Daughter of Claud Hunter, United States Air Force, Korean Theater

Whoever said the "sky is the limit" never came to Texas; in our state, there is no limit.

Kay Bailey Hutchison
United States Senator

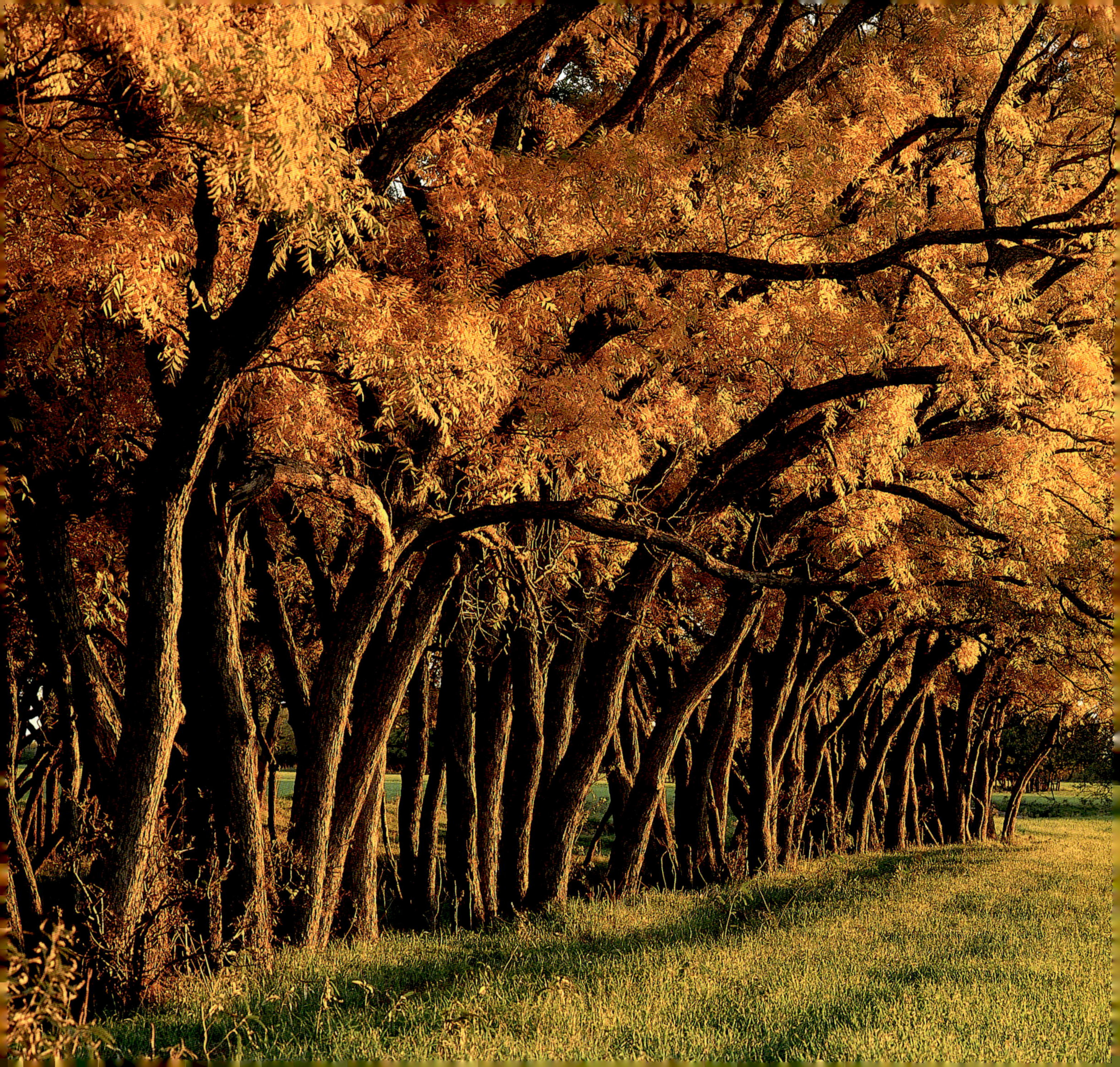

I must say as to what I have seen of Texas, it is the garden spot of the world, the best land and the best prospects for health I ever saw, and I do believe it is a fortune to any man to come here.

Davy Crockett
Frontiersman and Texas Revolutionary

Overleaf:

In Texas, the sky ignites at sunset and again at dawn, and in between are countless millions upon millions of sparkling jewels floating in a field of soft, dark velvet. Both at dawn and at sunset, shadows are long, and the meadows and fields and plains and mountains and sea shores are as colorful as a painter's palette. I fall in love with it again every day.

Bill Worrell
Texas Artist

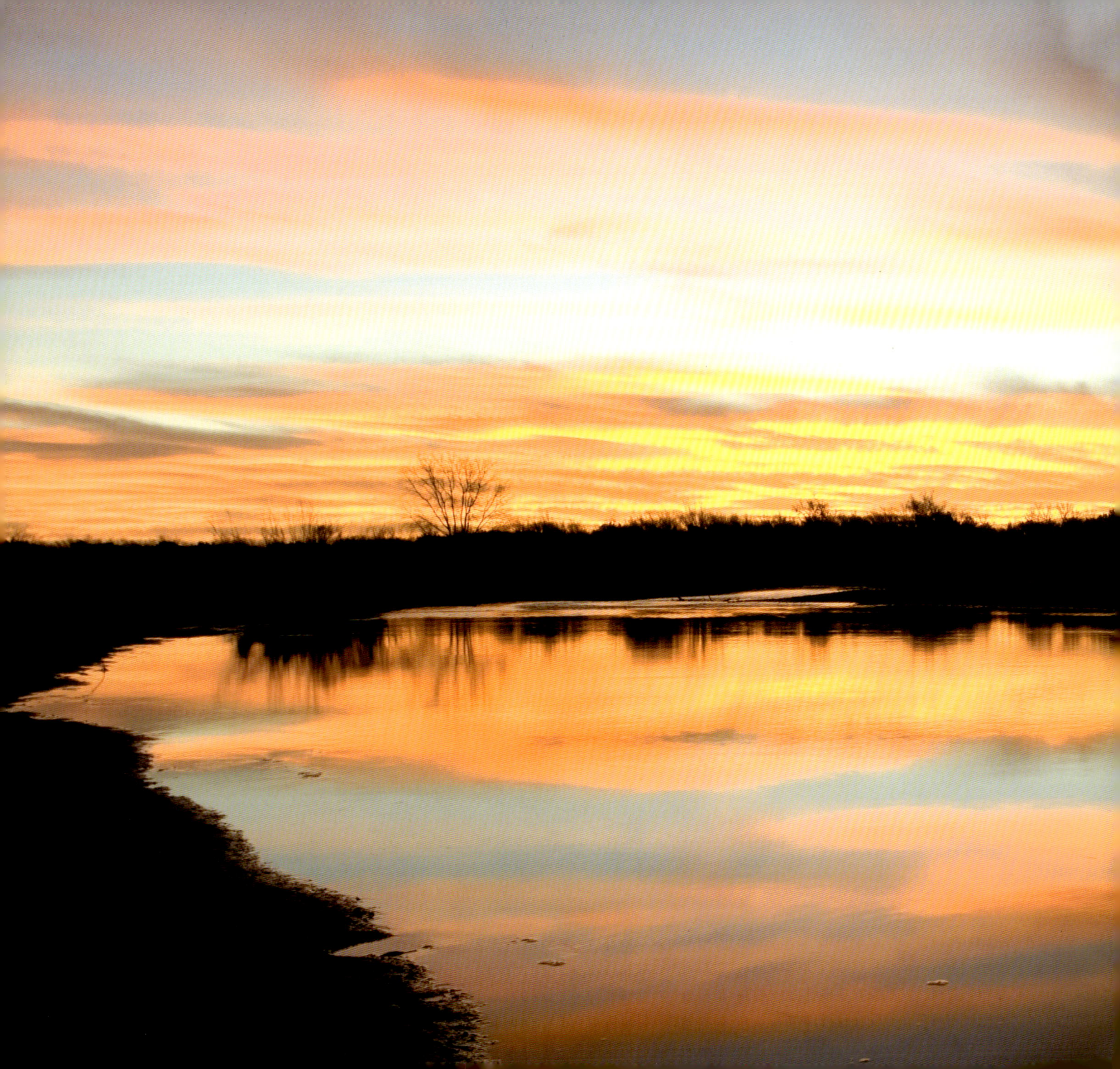

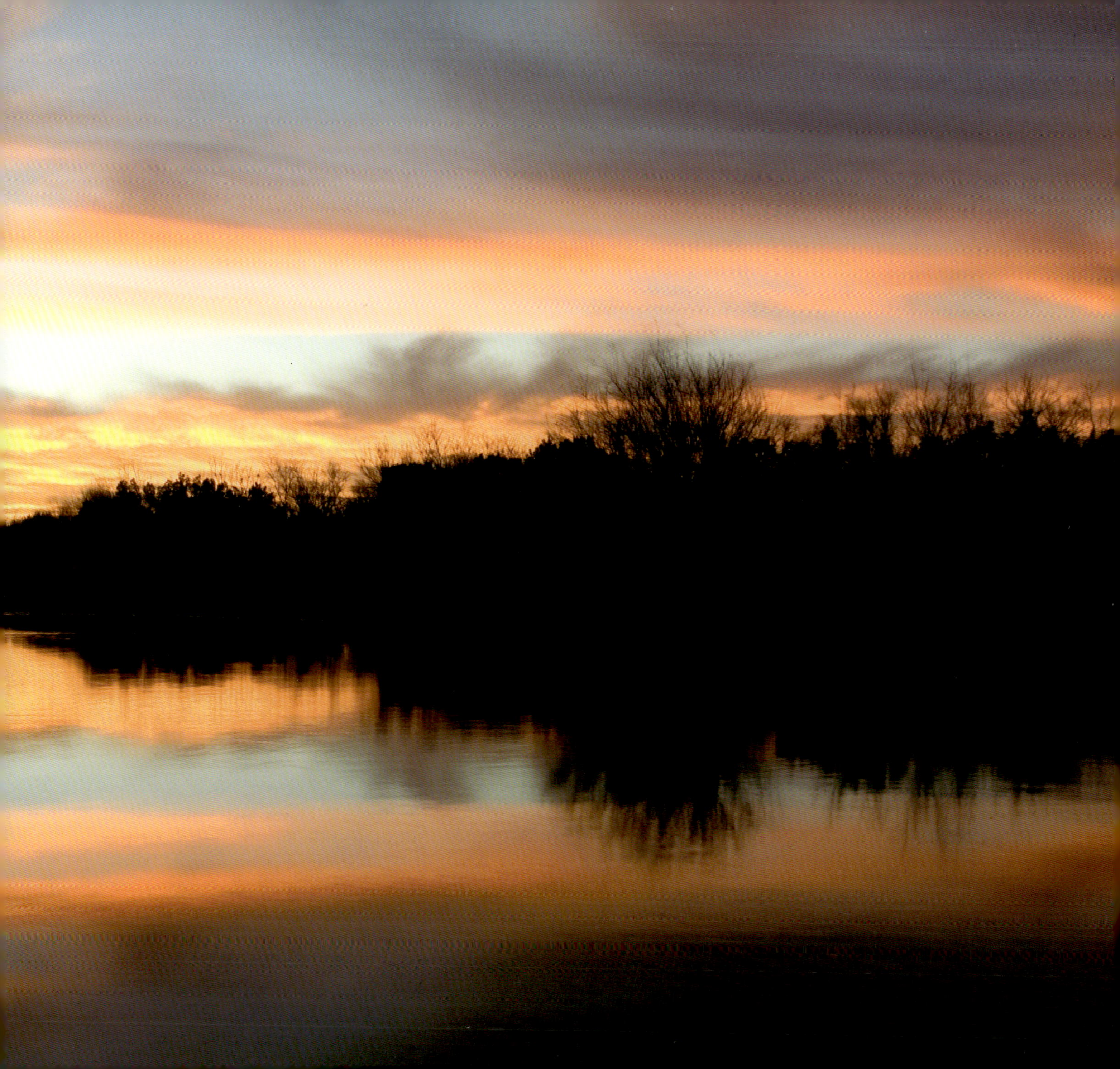

But ask the beasts, and they will teach you; Who among these does not know that the hand of the Lord has done this. In His hand is the life of every living thing and the breath of all mankind.

Job 12:7, 9-10

Texas is not just where we live, it's our life and our attitude. God Bless Texas.

Richard L. "Rick" Hardcastle
Texas State Representative

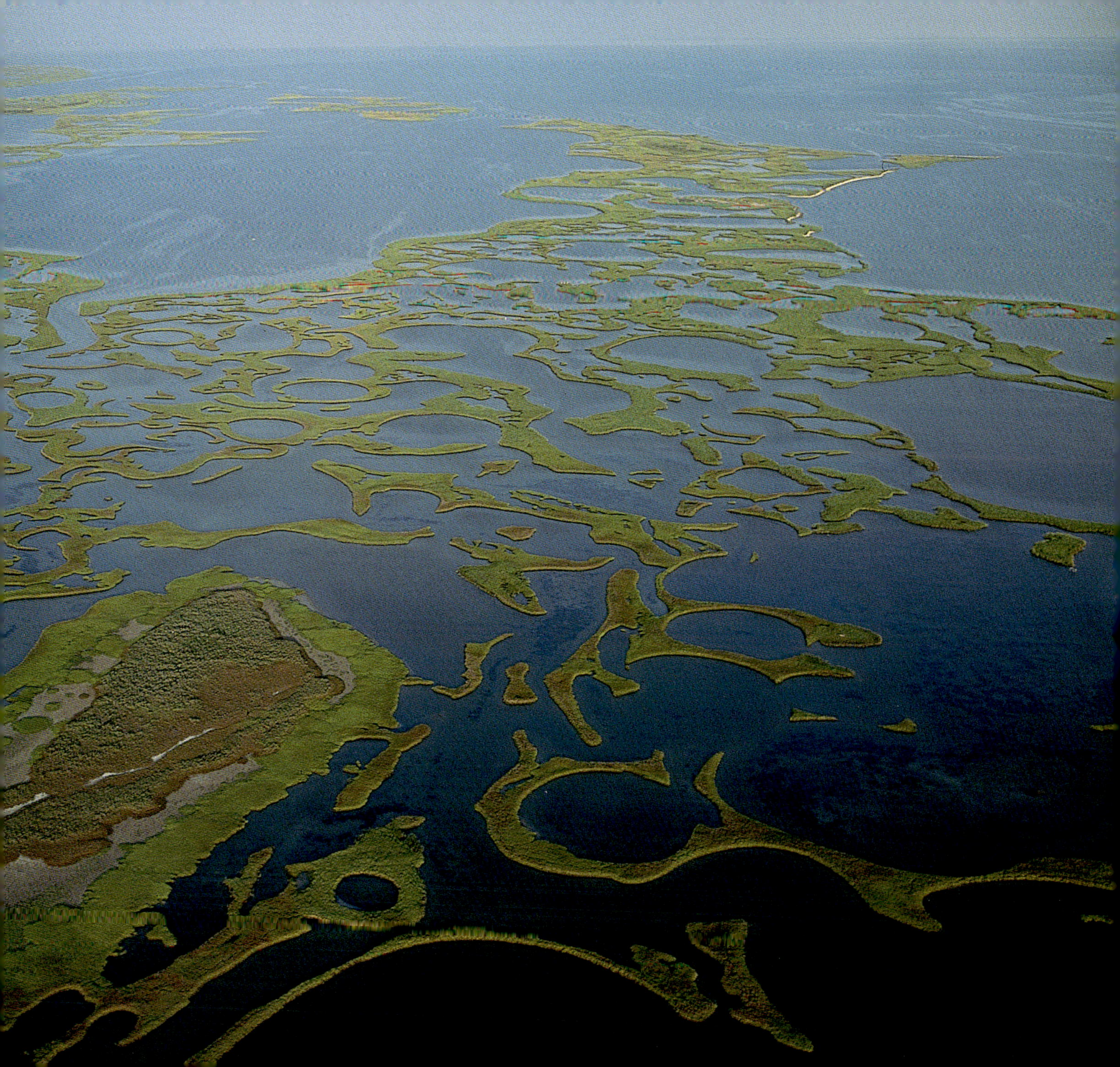

If you've ever scrambled atop Mount Livermore high in the Davis Mountains, paddled among the submerged cypress trees in Caddo Lake, or watched the whooping cranes glide through the marshes off Matagorda Island, you'll know why Texans love Texas so. Our lands and waters are simply without equal. Ensuring that these special places endure is one of the greatest gifts we can give to the future citizens of our beloved state.

Carter Smith
Executive Director, Texas Parks and Wildlife

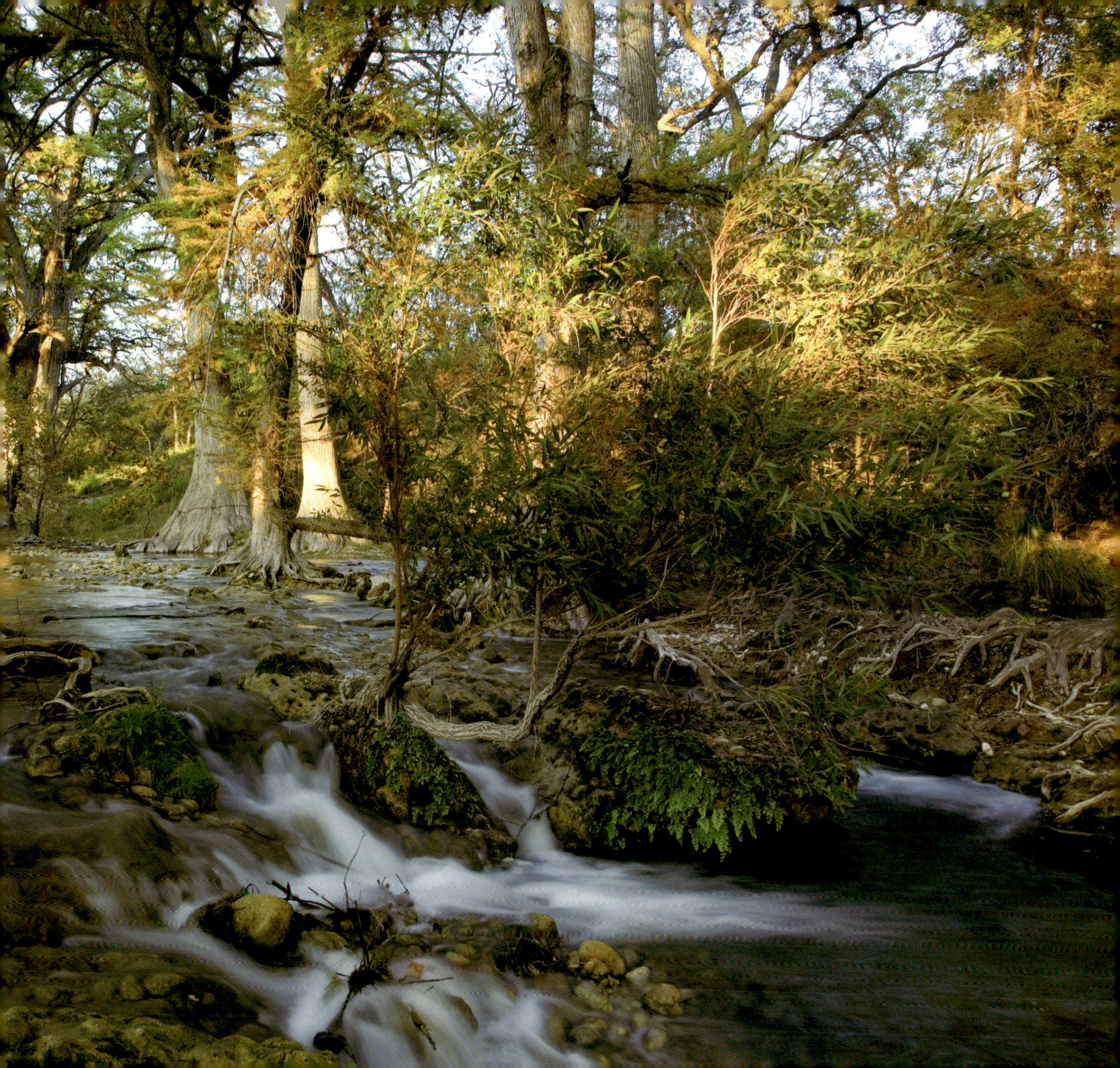

I lift up my eyes to the hills–
Where does my help come from?
My help comes from the Lord,
the Maker of heaven and earth.

Psalm 121:1-2
Inspiration for Doug Hawthorne

I grew up in the Panhandle of Texas where the wind blows all the time. However, the Panhandle is the most beautiful place on earth when she's got her Sunday britches on. But she can be brutal in the winter. The finest people on this planet live in the Panhandle of Texas. I remember growing up listening to the great historian, Laura V. Hamner, on KGNC radio in Amarillo. I'll never forget her closing remark after every show; "This is Laura V. Hamner reminding you that the Panhandle of Texas is the grandest spot on earth."
I believed her then. I believe her now.

Red Steagall
Cowboy Poet, "The Fence that Me and Shorty Built"

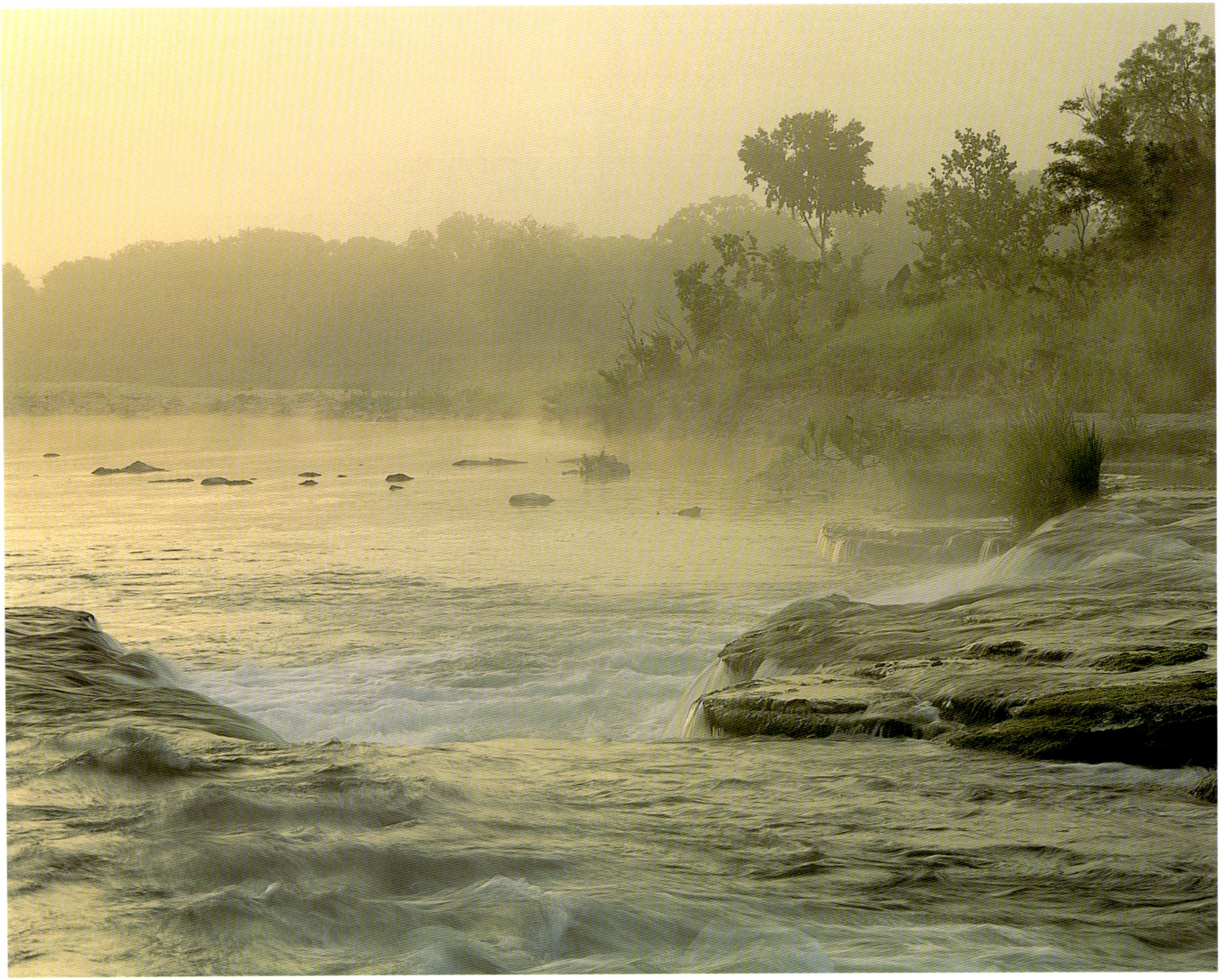

Those of us who have spent our lives in Texas and who have deep family roots here understand why Texas is the greatest place on earth. These images brilliantly capture the magnificent beauty of our natural bounty and geography. Generations of Texans will enjoy and treasure forever the grandeur of these timeless portrayals.

John Massey

I see Texas as the place of big dreams and quiet miracles. A place where anybody from any background or any community can scale heights as improbable as they are breathtaking.

David Dewhurst
Lt. Governor of Texas

Purge me and I shall be clean,
wash me and I will be white as snow.

    The Psalm of King David

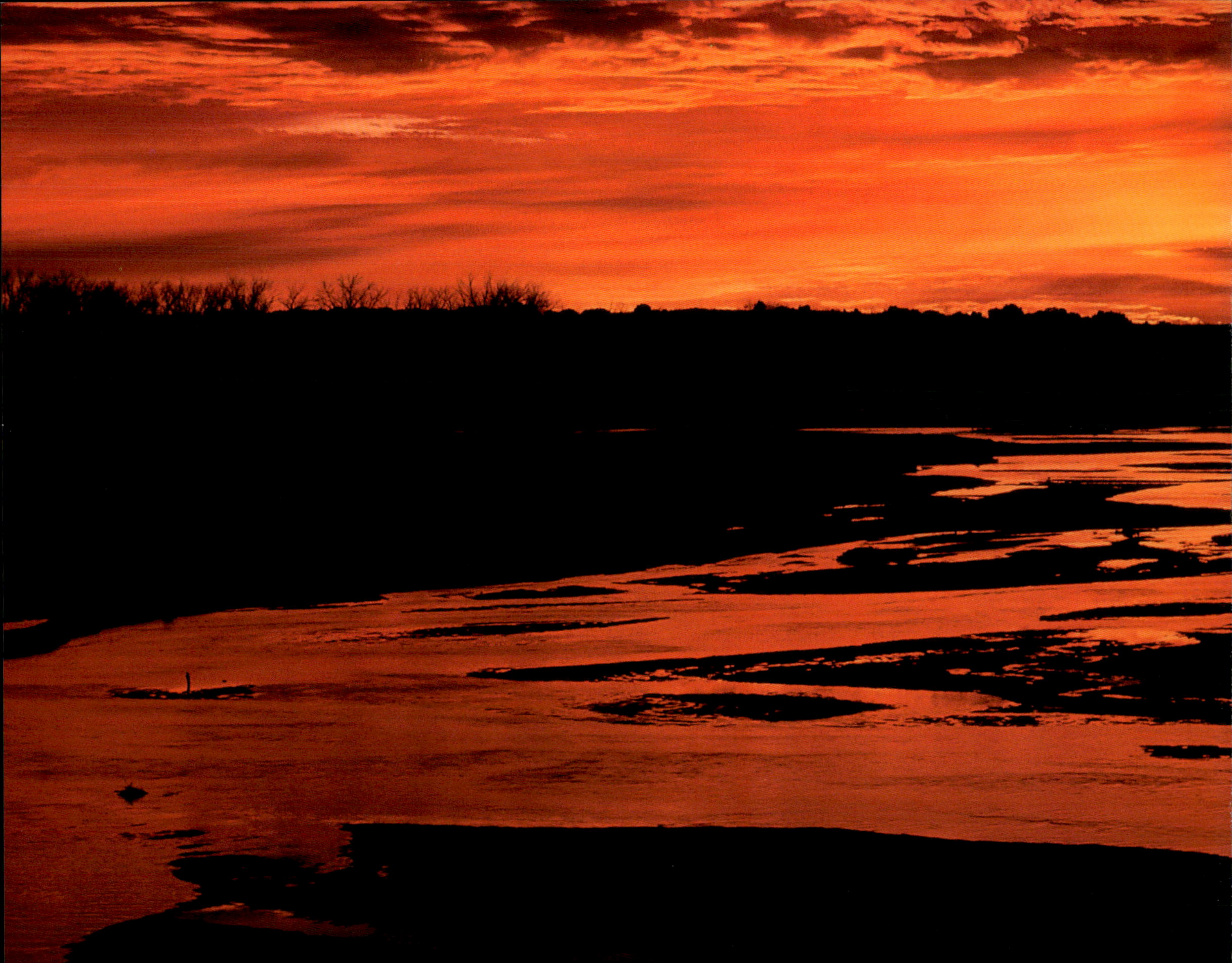

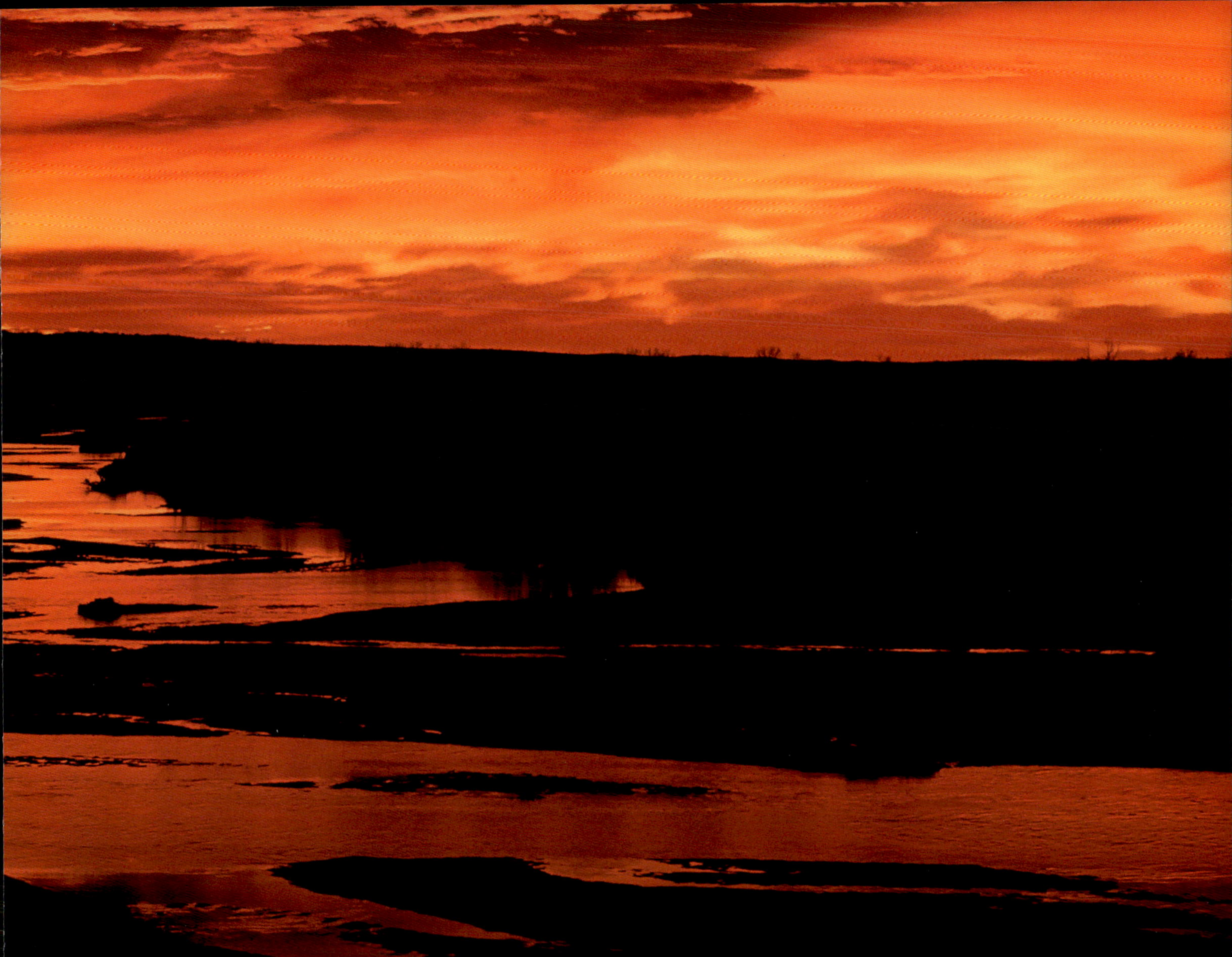

Whereas ye know not what shall be on the morrow. For what is life? It is even a vapour, that appeareth for a little time, and then vanisheth away.

James 4:14

Overleaf:

Ramon Adams, in his classic, "The Cowman & His Code of Ethics," described a dependable hand with the expression, "He'll do to ride the river with." It was high praise. It spoke of the kind of companion you could trust to help you move a herd across a swollen river. The phrase is pure Texas, and I think of it when I choose those with whom I associate. Such a quality is essential in a friend.

J. Philip Ferguson

Today, when people are so frantically seeking heroes, they need to look no further than here to find them in the 500 years of heroic conduct by Texans of all genders, races, and creeds. Texas has a history so rich and colorful that if written as fiction, it would be discarded as beyond belief.

J.P. Bryan

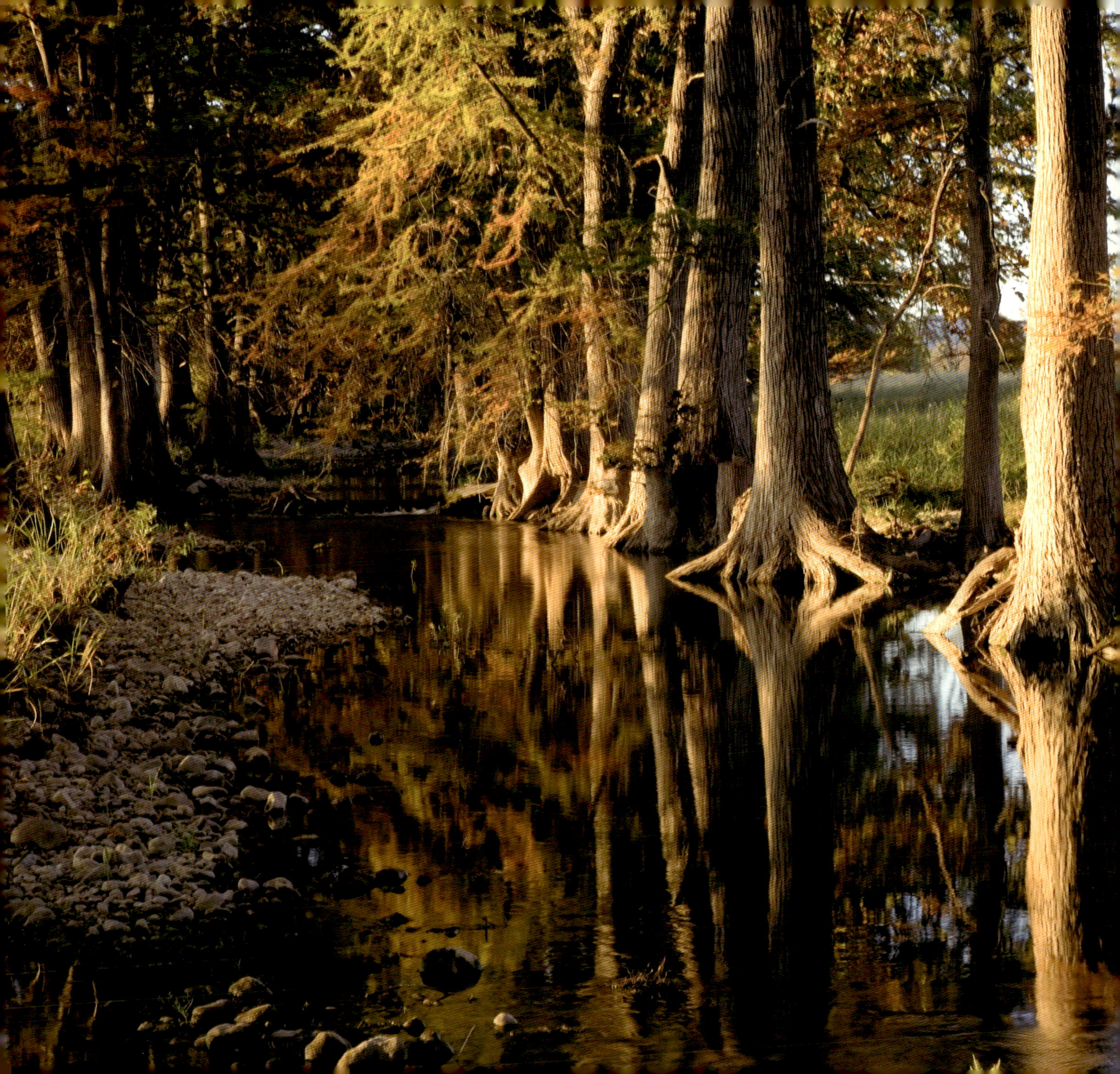

I am inspired by Texas' bounty of diverse natural resources found in its Trans Pecos; its tall pine forests, its Gulf Coast region; its Tall, Mid, and Short Grass Prairies; and its High and Rolling Plains. I am inspired by Texans both past and present: Native Americans who lived on its resources long before it was Texas and the explorers who told us all about its riches; the heroes of the Alamo, Goliad, and San Jacinto that won our right to be Texans; cattle barons, trail drivers, and hardy pioneers from which I sprung. All of whom built the myth and legend that is Texas.

Larry Butler
Former Texas State Conservationist
USDA Natural Resources Conservation Service

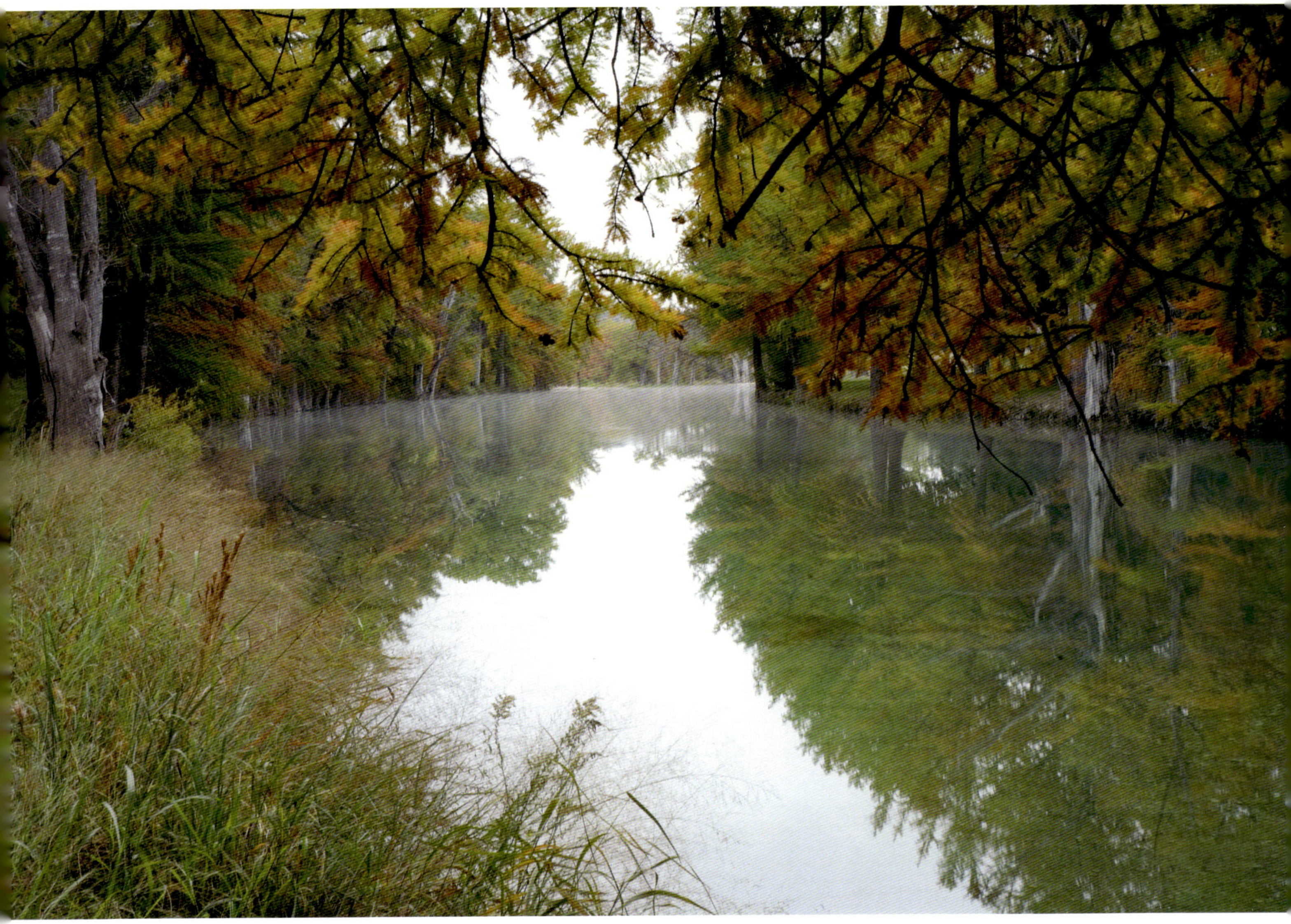

Texas has afforded me the opportunity to grow up learning to hunt, fish, handle a horse, and know a man's word is sealed with his handshake and a man always keeps his word. I've been horseback during the worst hailstorm you can imagine, and I've seen the most beautiful sunsets on God's Earth. I've picked wild plums with my wife Jean and helped her make jelly. I've plowed the soil. Texas has given all of this to me. Everything I am or hope to be is because I am a Texan.

J. Martin Basinger

Overleaf:

There are a lot of interesting characters in Texas.

Teel Bivins
United States Ambassador

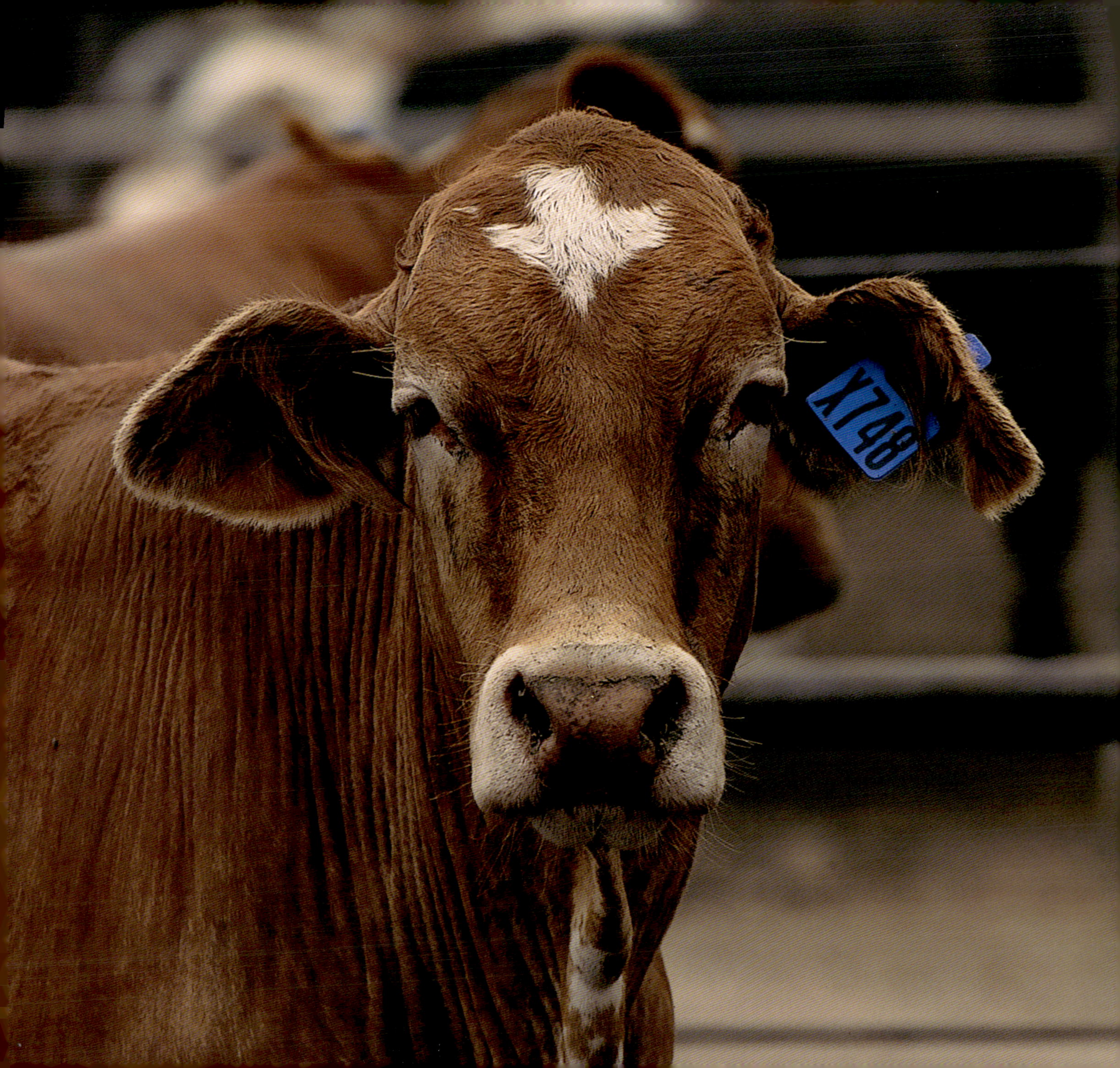
X748

Photography Technical Information

Jacket Front: Canon F1N with Canon 14mm f/2.8 L, Fujichrome Velvia 50 ISO
Guadalupe Sand Dunes, Dell City
Back: Hasselblad 501CM with Zeiss 80mm f/2.8 Planar, Fujichrome Velvia 50 ISO
State Capitol, Austin

ii Hasselblad 501CM with Zeiss 50mm f/4 Distagon, Fujichrome Velvia 100 ISO
Llano River, Junction

vi Canon EOS 5D with Canon 400mm f/5.6 L, 100 ISO
Chinati Mountains, Marfa

xiv Canon EOS 5D with Canon 24-105mm f/4 L IS, 100 ISO
Highway 82, Knox County

2 Hasselblad 501CM with Zeiss 150mm f/4 Sonnar, Fujichrome Velvia 50 ISO
Between Fort Davis and Valentine

4 Canon F1N with Canon 80-200 f/4, Fujichrome Velvia 50 ISO
Ceiling of State Capitol, Austin

5 Canon EOS 5D with 24-105mm f/4 L IS, 100 ISO
Ross Ranch, King County

6 Canon EOS 5D with 24-105mm f/4 L IS, 100 ISO
Highway 82, west of Benjamin

9 Hasselblad 501CM with Zeiss 50mm f/4 Distagon, Fujichrome Velvia 50 ISO
El Capitan, Guadalupe Mountains

10 Hasselblad 501CM with Zeiss 80mm f/2.8 Planar, Fujichrome Velvia 50 ISO
San Antonio Canyon, Chinati Mountains

11 Hasselblad 501CM with Zeiss 150mm f/4 Sonnar, Fujichrome Velvia 50 ISO
Texas State Cemetery, Austin

12-13 Canon F1N with Canon 500mm f/4.5 L, Fujichrome Velvia 50 ISO
Outskirts of Amarillo

14 Canon F1N with Canon 14mm f/2.8 L, Fujichrome Velvia 50 ISO
Between Marfa and Presidio

15 Hasselblad 501CM with Zeiss 80mm f/2.8 Planar, Fujichrome Velvia 50 ISO
San Jacinto Monument, La Porte

17 Canon F1N with Canon 500mm f/4.5 L, Fujichrome Velvia 50 ISO
Knox County

18 Hasselblad 501CM with Zeiss 50mm f/4 Distagon, Fujichrome Velvia 50 ISO
Fort McKavett State Historical Site

19 Canon EOS 5D with Canon 400mm f/5.6 L, 100 ISO
Highway 82, west of Benjamin

20-21 Canon EOS 5D with Canon TS-E 24mm f/3.5 L, 50 ISO
Dolan Falls on the Devil's River

22 Hasselblad 501CM with Zeiss 50mm f/4 Distagon, Fujichrome Velvia 50 ISO
Possum Kingdom Lake

24-25 Canon EOS 1D Mark II with Canon 400mm f/5.6 L, 400 ISO
6666 Ranch, King County

27 Canon F1N with Canon 500mm f/4.5 L, Fujichrome Velvia 50 ISO
South of San Antonio

28 Canon EOS 5D with 70-200mm f/2.8 L, 100 ISO
Interstate 10, west of Junction

29 Canon EOS 1D Mark IIN with Canon 400mm f/5.6 L, 100 ISO
Bayou, near Orange

30 Canon EOS 1N with Canon 17-35mm f/2.8 L, Fujichrome Velvia 50 ISO
Canadian River bottom, north of Adrian

32 Canon EOS 5D with Canon 24-105mm f/4 L IS, 100 ISO
Cibolo Creek Ranch, south of Marfa

33 Canon EOS 5D with Canon 300mm f/4 L, 100 ISO
Interstate 44, southwest of Dallas

34 Canon F1N with Canon 20-35mm f/3.5 L, Fujichrome 100 ISO
Canadian River, west of Amarillo

36-37 Canon EOS 5D with Canon 16-35mm f/2.8 L, 50 ISO
Cemetery, Shafter

38 Canon EOS 5D with Canon 16-35mm f/2.8 L, 50 ISO
Mason County

39	Canon EOS 5D with Canon 16-35mm f/2.8 L, 50 ISO *Mason County*	
40	Hasselblad 501CM with Zeiss 50mm f/4 Distagon, Fujichrome 50 ISO *Texas Declaration of Independence*	
42	Hasselblad 501CM with Zeiss 150mm f/4 Sonnar, Fujichrome Velvia 50 ISO *Mission Concepcion, San Antonio*	
43	Hasselblad Flex Body with 50mm f/4 Distagon, Fujichrome Velvia 50 ISO *Wheat field, north of Benjamin*	
44	Canon EOS 5D with Canon 24-105mm f/4 L IS, 100 ISO *Badlands, north of Benjamin*	
45	Canon EOS 5D with Canon TS-E 24mm f/3.5 L, 400 ISO *Catholic Church, Rhineland*	
47	Canon F1N with Canon 20-35mm f/3.5 L, Fujichrome 50 ISO *The Alamo, San Antonio*	
48	Canon EOS 1N with Canon 17-35mm f/2.8 L, Fujichrome Velvia 50 ISO *Rolling Plains, west of Benjamin*	
50	Canon EOS 5D with Canon 24-105mm f/4 L IS, 160 ISO *East Rim of Palo Duro Canyon, Canyon*	
51	Canon EOS 1D Mark II with Canon 16-35mm f/2.8 L, 50 ISO *6666 Ranch, King County*	
52	Canon F1N with Canon 80-200mm f/4, Fujichrome Velvia 50 ISO *Aerial of Brazos River, Knox County*	
55	Canon EOS 5D with Canon 16-35mm f/2.8 L, 50 ISO *Cumulus Mammatus, west of Benjamin*	
56	Canon EOS 5D with Canon 24-105mm f/4 L IS, 100 ISO *9/11 Memorial, Texas Tech University*	
57	Canon EOS 5D with Canon 24-105mm f/4 L IS, 100 ISO *Striated clouds, Knox County*	
58	Hasselblad 501CM with Zeiss 150mm f/4 Sonnar, Fujichrome Velvia 50 ISO *Soap Berry Trees, Knox County*	
60-61	Canon EOS 1D Mark II with Canon 16-35mm f/2.8 L, 50 ISO *Wichita River, Baylor County*	
62	Canon F1N with Canon 500mm f/4.5 L, Fujichrome Velvia 50 ISO *Coyote, King County*	
63	Canon F1N with Canon 28-85mm f/4, Fujichrome Velvia 50 ISO *Gulf estruaries, near Corpus Christi*	
65	Canon EOS 5D with Canon 24-105mm f/4 L IS, 100 ISO *Sabinal River, near Utopia*	
66	Canon EOS 1N with Canon 70-200 f/2.8 L, Fujichrome Velvia 50 ISO *Desert fog, Big Bend Ranch State Park*	
67	Canon F1N with Canon 14mm f/2.8 L, Fujichrome Velvia 50 ISO *Rolling Plains, Knox County*	
68	Hasselblad 501CM with Zeiss 150mm f/4 Sonnar, Fujichrome Velvia 50 ISO *Llano River, Junction*	
70	Canon EOS 5D with Canon 24-105mm f/4 L IS, 100 ISO *Ghost town, Shafter*	
71	Hasselblad 501CM with Zeiss 150mm f/4 Sonnar, Fujichrome Velvia 50 ISO *Snow cover, north of Benjamin*	
72-73	Canon F1N with Canon 80-200 f/4, Fujichrome Velvia 50 ISO *Red River, north of Turkey*	
74	Canon EOS 5D with Canon 24-105mm f/4 L IS, 100 ISO *Autumn fog, Canadian River bottom*	
75	Canon EOS 5D with 70-200mm f/2.8 L, 100 ISO *Eagle Canyon, Langtry*	
76	Canon EOS 5D with Canon 24-105mm f/4 L IS, 100 ISO *Sabinal River, near Utopia*	
78	Canon EOS 5D with Canon 24-105mm f/4 L IS, 100 ISO *Sabinal River, north of Utopia*	
80	Canon F1N with Canon 500mm f/4.5 L, Fujichrome Velvia 50 *Stockyards, near Hereford*	